SHE DATED THE ASSHATS, BUT MARRIED THE GOOD GUY

SHE DATED THE ASSHATS, BUT MARRIED THE GOOD GUY

"How to Go from Toxic Love to Real Love in 12 Exercises"

SHANNON BRADLEY-COLLEARY

ISBN-13: 9781540469632
ISBN-10: 1540469638

RAVES FOR THIS BOOK

Kate Green MS, NCC, LPC says:

"*She Dated the Asshats, but Married the Good Guy* is an incredible read in which Shannon provides enjoyment and insight.

"Her thoughtful recounting of clients' stories draws the reader in, illustrates, and simplifies - as much as is possible - a complicated emotional process.

"Realizing who truly deserves our commitment and love (ourselves always, as Shannon often reminds the reader) can be uncomfortable and scary; realizing what we deserve in a relationship and accepting our lack of control over others – even more so.

"Shannon is patient and encouraging with the reader because she speaks from experience and a place of compassion.

"Boundaries, respect, sexuality, learning to love and accept oneself after trauma, seeking support – Shannon doesn't shy away from anything needed to unpack what has been making life and relationships painful, and the work that needs to be done on the reader's journey towards Real Love."

Vicki P. says:

"Shannon's book helped me finally realize why I was still dating Asshats. Understanding codependency and how to change its hold on me was eye-opening.

"Her book gives clear concise steps to empower you to have the best life possible.

"Shannon does this in a humorous, non-judgmental, and loving way. This book was a life-changing read for me! I highly recommend it to anyone struggling with self-esteem and relationship issues."

Claudia Lewis MA, LMFT Psychotherapy and EMDR says:

"Shannon engages the reader in a humorous exploration of how to turn around toxic dating habits. Using her own life experience, she offers a witty and practical guide to identify unhealthy patterns and move closer to finding the love you want."

Carol C. says:

"This book is pure gold for every woman who has ever wondered why all the men she dates are jerks and what she can do about it.

"This book debunks all the so-called 'relationship improvement' instructions by big name 'experts' and offers women a reality check and excellent advice to help them find and be successful in a functional relationship."

Debra Ellis Smith, Licensed Clinical Mental Health Counselor, LCMHC says:

"*She Dated the Asshats, But Married the Good Guy* contains practical advice and assignments to recognize red flags. I liked Shannon's willingness to share her own experiences with readers ... It's just a great book."

Gayle Tribe, M.Ed, PPS says:

"A comprehensive guide full of insight, wit and concrete tips on how to kick toxic relationships for good and find true contentment with oneself and others."

Lisa W. says:

"I loved this book. It was a game-changer for me! I thought if I just avoided Asshats my troubles would be over. It never occurred to me that I had to change more than just my attitude towards men.

"On behalf of the women who will benefit from your book I just want to say thank you!"

America P. says:

"I think that anyone who is struggling and serious about changing the dynamics in their current and/or future relationships should read this book! I did not want to put it down.

"I related to Shannon's humor, her compassion for all parties involved, her point of view and her experience on the subject.

"I have attended numerous seminars and read my fair share of self-help books over the last several years, I found Shannon's to be insightful, comprehensive and practical, even if one is not ready to move on [from a toxic relationship] just yet.

"In short, I received some real gems the first time I read it and plan to read it again. Thank you, Shannon, for sharing your experience and wisdom."

Kathryn M. says:

"An entertainingly clever guide to the Asshats disguised, however briefly, as Good Men.

"This is not a man-bashing fluff-piece, so gird your loins for some uncomfortable squirming as the sensation of familiarity creeps up your spine.

"Using real-life stories, straight-talk and useful exercises, Colleary helps readers not only rid themselves of an Asshat, but understand why they became involved with one in the first place.

"Read, think, act, and be on your healthy way to recovery. Watch out Asshats, you've been rooted out of the woodpile."

Marie C. says:

"Wow ... just wow. While my childhood was reasonably normal and loving, somewhere in my first marriage to my childhood sweetheart/Asshat my world changed. I became co-dependent and a people-pleaser.

"Our marriage was a 23-year train wreck of verbal and psychological abuse towards me, and our kids and I was simply not prepared emotionally to walk away from it

"Shannon - how I wish I'd read this book when I was 25 instead of 65!!!!

"I wish everyone who finds themselves in these untenable relationships could read your book and learn how to turn on their heels and RUN the other way and get help in recovering from the damage!

"It doesn't matter if it is a dating relationship, a cohabitating relationship or a marriage.

"Thank you so much for your willingness to share your vulnerability and your wisdom. Thank you a thousand times!!!"

Lisa C. says:

"Having been married to one Asshat and having ended a relationship with another, I only wish I had this book 20 years ago!

"Asshats come in a variety of flavors, and this guide gives a breakdown of characteristics so we can recognize them before we get sucked into their never-ending games.

"Written with plenty of humor and real-life examples, *She Dated the Asshats, But Married the Good Guy* offers healthy solutions to discover our own strength and leave that Asshat behind for good.

"Shannon's empowering message is that we all deserve Real Love and respect and she counsels that 'a relationship is only as good as the person who tries the least.' Think about that one!"

Alexandra Williams, MA, Agency Counseling with an emphasis on Marriage and Family says:

"I was curious about how Colleary would present her information, hoping she wouldn't fall into the trap of armchair psychology or preachy tell-all.

"I was happily surprised to discover she has found a perfect balance of research, anecdotes, encouragement and suggestions.

"The overall non-judgmental tone makes this a perfect read for any woman trying to find support in making changes in her relationships."

Wendy N. says:

"This is exactly what I needed to read. Shannon's book is a wonderful complement to the work I've been doing after having my life Asshat-ered.

"*She Dated the Asshats, But Married the Good Guy* is straightforward, it is practical and refreshingly honest, which is priceless after all the crazy-making."

Mona A. says:

"Written with the same friendly, fun-to-read voice that Shannon's readers have come to know and love, *She Dated the Asshats, But Married the Good Guy* is well-organized and broken down into easy-to-implement actionable steps.

"If *Real Love* is what you're looking for, you have to read this book!"

TABLE OF CONTENTS

IS THIS BOOK FOR YOU?

Raise your hand if any of the following statements apply to you:

1. You've been on stakeout at 3 a.m. outside your man's apartment because you think he might be cheating.
2. You've snooped through his cell phone, computer, desk, car or underwear drawer to find evidence of infidelity.
3. You date and fall in love with men who are emotionally unavailable.
4. You're just someone's booty call. (And don't want to be!)
5. You give and give in your relationship to a man who doesn't reciprocate or respect you.
6. You have expectations your man can't or won't fulfill, which leads to disappointment.
7. You can't maintain healthy boundaries with your guy around sex, money and time.
8. You feel like you must control, save or rescue your guy.
9. You have too much empathy for him, while he has little to none for you.
10. You abandon yourself and your values to keep your man.

11. Your relationship makes you feel insecure, sad, lonely, anxious, angry, resentful, ashamed and/or embarrassed.
12. You've caught your man cheating.
13. You want your relationship to get healthy or you want the strength to leave.
14. You manage to leave, but he comes back when you're finally feeling strong and you go back to him.
15. You want to get married, have kids or simply have a monogamous commitment, but worry this will never happen for you.

If these questions resonated, then this book is for you.

Chances are you're already in a relationship with an Asshat or are vulnerable to attracting another one. And I should know.

I spent a total of 10 years in two long-term relationships with toxic, emotionally abusive men I'll henceforth refer to as The Greek God and Mister Cruelly Handsome.

These relationships included stalking, begging, crying, gnashing of teeth, flailing, threatening, seducing, tap-dancing sans appropriate footwear, butt kissing … and that was just on my end!

This was before I turned it around and became a magnet for kind, committed, generous Real Love.

I'm going to walk you through every exercise I completed in this book so you can do the same.

It's going to revolutionize your life!

ASSHATS, JET FUEL & "REAL LOVE"

Women who attract and stay in toxic relationships tend to have two tragic flaws that make it extremely difficult for them to leave.

1. An Overabundance of Empathy
2. Misplaced Responsibility

This is especially true of women who grew up in homes with divorce, drug and alcohol addiction or immature, needy parents.

For this reason I prefer to use a word to describe toxic partners that might seem derogatory, but is helpful to Women Who Love Too Much. That word is:

ASSHAT [as-hat] noun, vulgar: A person who wears his ass upon his head like a hat.

I also use these synonyms:

* Heartbreaker
* Toxic Guy
* Rake

* Skirt Chaser
* Womanizer
* Lothario
* Casanova
* Narcissist
* Mayhaps Shit Weasel?

Okay, I won't use Shit Weasel, but I'll be sorely tempted. *Sorely tempted!*

Using the word "Asshat" might seem mean and *not* in keeping with Equal-Pay-For-Equal-Work feminism, but more along the lines of We-Hate-Men feminism.

It's not meant to be wrathful. It's simply a descriptor for someone who can wreak havoc in our lives if we let them.

Here's the thing about Asshats. We don't have to judge or revile them. They are, quite simply, damaged people.

And by the way, Asshat isn't a gender specific word.

<u>Confession</u>: *I* was an Asshat in one of my relationships with a kind, unsuspecting man.

At that time in my life, "kind" equaled "boring." I was immature and damaged and needed to get my shizz together.

I basically used this sweet fellow, whom I'll call Oliver, as a place-holder until the next Asshat could come along in his Toyota Celica and sweep me off my feet.

So I really don't have anything against Asshats per se, except for this:

<u>They Steal Our Jet Fuel</u>

I believe we're all born with a full tank of jet fuel that propels us through life.

The problem is, when we love heartbreakers they can drain our jets by lying, cheating, criticizing and committing other chicanery.

So instead of having a full tank at our disposal, we waste precious fuel trying to change and control our man.

My Jets

Twenty years ago, I was an actress. I'd been paid to perform in five music videos and five plays. I'd booked two movies (one in which I played the lead), and four television roles.

I was bi-coastal for five months, playing the lead in a revival of William Inge's classic play, *Picnic*, at a prestigious theater in Connecticut.

Then I met Mr. Cruelly Handsome.

Over the next five years of our relationship I booked only one national commercial and one guest-starring role on an episode of a television show, which was almost immediately cancelled after my appearance.

(That Asshat Billy Bob Thornton co-starred. Coincidence?)

At that time, I also wanted to find a husband, get married and start a family.

It seemed the more jet fuel I used to move Mister C.H. toward *that* particular future with me, the further I travelled from my heartfelt desire.

When I finally unclenched my fist, and let that toxic relationship go, suddenly the needle on my gauge pinged "full." All my jets were on fire.

Here's what happened next:

* I realized it was time to quit chasing the acting dream. Closing that door opened a window to a new career as a writer.

* I wrote plays, three of which were produced within months of each other.
* I was accepted into and completed an MFA degree in UCLA's exclusive screenwriting program.
* I signed with William Morris Endeavor, the largest literary agency in the world.
* I sold my first screenplay to Warner Brothers for six figures and quit my waitressing job.
* I landed a succession of other screenwriting jobs for Disney, Fox and Lifetime.
* I met and married my husband.
* I became a homeowner.
* I gave birth to two hilarious, smart, beloved daughters.
* In the safe harbor of a loving relationship I continued my journey of my own personal growth.

And guess what? All of this happened within six years. Just *one year* longer than my dead-end toxic relationship with Mister C.H.

Judging vs. Judgment

So, while we can choose not to *judge* Asshats, as we have not walked one hundred miles in their moccasins, we must have good *judgment* about them and the space we allow them to hold in our lives.

Real Love vs. True Love

The goal of reading and working the exercises and tasks in this book is to vanquish the Asshats and invite Real Love into our lives, *not* True Love.

True Love is for children.

I don't know about you, but I spent my pubescent years reading Gothic bodice-rippers.

The stories often began when a prisoner, named something like Roark De Lafontaine, escaped the London gaol. Often he was secretly a Marquis or Viscount who'd been kidnapped and framed for murder!

Roark would flee across the moors upon his noble steed, Jericho or Firebolt, who would respond *only* to Roark's high-pitched, sonar whistle. (Bloodhounds could hear it too!)

Just *inches* from freedom, Roark would collide with a carriage bearing the sumptuous, virginal heroine of our tale, Lady Shanna or Countess Jezebel Tremaine.

Roark tended to wear snug breeches that covered his steel-hewn thighs and bulging manhood. His crystalline azure eyes bored into Jezzie's very soul.

Roark risked recapture because he couldn't resist this virgin vixen, ultimately divesting her of her clothes and maidenhood in a molten-hot lava-parade of sexual explosions.

Basically, Hotness and Horniness became my definition of True Love.

And *boy* did I want to get me some. Sigh.

Granted, the two rogues I spent 10 years loving *did* look a great deal like Roark. But it was a rude awakening to learn that, during that time, I was *not* the only woman to discover what was under those snug breeches.

Apparently "True Love" can include more than two people!

"Real Love" is for adults.

It *can* include plenty of great sex. But it's not defined by sex. It's constant, committed and patient.

Off With Your Knickers, Royal Lady!

It survives sickness, stock market downturns, horrible bosses and children who never sleep, hearing every move you make at 120,000 Hz, like vampire bats.

Real Love can even survive post-natal hemorrhoids.

Yes, I know *you* don't have hemorrhoids and that your pristine bottom is beyond reproach, but I just want you to know that Real Love can ride out ignominies like hemorrhoids. Post-birthing two babies I know of which I speak.

So Real Love is what we're looking for.

And how do we get there? Before we can boot the Asshats from our lives, we must first be able to spot them.

BE THE WOMAN WHO *DIDN'T* ANSWER THE DOOR

When I first heard the following story, I didn't get it. Now I recognize that the woman in this story shined a light for me to follow on my path to relationship awesomeness.

Without further ado:

Julia's Story

While we were dating, Mister Cruelly Handsome told me the story of a "bitch" he tried to date a few months before we met. We'll call her Julia.

Mister C.H. met Julia in a bar and was instantly attracted to her.

He came on strong, flattering her, lavishing her with attention, practically getting on his knees to beg for her phone number. She happily complied (the lad was a looker).

Mister C.H. called Julia right away and scheduled a date after his 5:30 end-of-shift at the police station.

He told Julia he'd swing home, shower up, change and then pick her up at 7:00 o'clock for dinner and clubbing later. She was delighted.

Five-thirty rolled around and Mister C.H's shift ended.

He thought about heading home to get ready for his date, but decided to give his truck a quick tune-up. It shouldn't take long.

By 6:30 he realized he was running late for his date with Julia. But he was making such good headway that he didn't want to stop just yet.

So, he called Julia and told her he'd been delayed by an "emergency." But he'd pick her up by 7:30.

Julia completely understood: heroism trumped timeliness.

Mister C.H. decided the phone call bought him just *a little more time* to finish up with his truck and to "shoot the shit" with a couple of his buddies working the following shift.

When his friends left to clock in, Mister C.H. noticed it had somehow become 7:45! Julia was probably wondering where the hell he was.

But, rather than feeling sheepish about losing track of time and disrespecting *her* time, Mister C.H. felt a little bit annoyed … *by Julia!*

He didn't like knowing she was waiting for him and decided he'd get to Julia's house when he got there. Which was 9 o'clock.

A Full Two Hours Later Than Originally Planned!

But, in his mind it was still early for dining and clubbing. So Mister C.H. stepped down from his now perfectly tuned truck and rang Julia's doorbell.

There was no answer. He rang the doorbell again. No answer. After ringing several times, Mister C.H. was fit to be tied.

I mean, *who did this girl think she was, standing <u>him</u> up this way? Didn't she know he was a Hot Cop drowning in Badge Bunnies?*

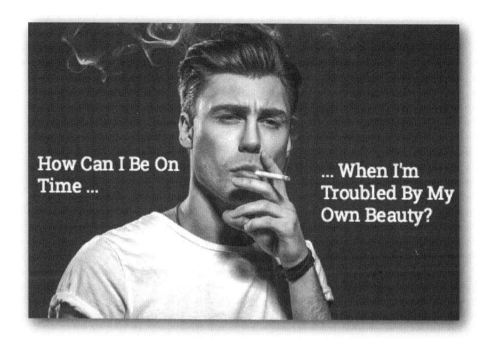

How Can I Be On Time ...

... When I'm Troubled By My Own Beauty?

He pulled out his phone and dialed Julia's number, wanting to know where she was and to give her an earful. She answered on the first ring.

"Where are you?" Mister C.H. spat. "I'm at your front door to pick you up for our date and you're not even here!"

"Actually, I *am* here," Julia informed him. "But I'm not going out with you tonight or any other night, for that matter."

"What're you talking about? I'm here. I have a really romantic dinner planned."

"Mister C.H.," she replied -- and I envy her poise -- "You're not interested enough in me for me to be interested in you. Don't come here again. And lose my phone number."

I believe that deserves its own marquee:

You're Not Interested Enough in Me for Me to Be Interested in You!

You go, girl! This drove Mister C.H. wild. Suddenly this woman was *sooo* desirable!

He was willing to do anything she asked at any time, in any amount. She told him she just wasn't interested and wished him well.

Julia knew something in *one night* that it took me five years in a relationship with the same chap to figure out. He thought of himself first, and other people last, if at all.

The fact that Mister C.H. saw himself as a victim in this tale should've been a red flag accompanied by a siren flashing lights.

But I had some learnin' to do. I had to create and work every exercise in this book and I *know* that sharing my path to relationship recovery will catalyze your learning curve.

HOW TO USE THIS BOOK

In Part One we'll identify "The Problem."

'll help you peel back the layers of the Denial Onion (yep, I just coined that phrase) so you can become more self-aware and accept the reality of your current circumstances.

> ### *It's Only Through Self-Awareness That We Can Change Ourselves, Hence Our Lives.*

You'll learn to determine what is and isn't your responsibility. What you can and *cannot* change and/or control.

In Part Two I'll walk you through The Solution.

Often we feel like we are victims of circumstances beyond our control. But there's always a way to get out of The Problem and into The Solution if we make up our minds to do it.

I offer 12 life-altering exercises that are your path to emotional freedom and a thriving (rather than surviving) future.

Here's a handy table that elucidates your learning outcomes as you read this book with an open mind and work the exercises.

The Problem	The Solution
1. You're attracted to men who use and disrespect you, or who are unavailable. You're also not sure what a healthy relationship looks like.	1. You follow a "Dating Plan" to attract an available, loving partner and instantly recognize toxic behavior. You have a clear vision of the partner you want.
2. You wonder if you're too demanding and think you're unworthy of the committed love you desire.	2. You know what issues are your partner's and which are yours. Even with your issues you know you deserve healthy love and feel entitled to it.
3. You talk, threaten, seduce, people-please and manipulate to change or control your romantic partner, but nothing works.	3. You ask for what you want/need directly and honestly, then let go of the results.
4. You self-abandon to please your romantic partner.	4. You stand tall, no longer self-abandoning. You maintain healthy boundaries.
5. You're embarrassed by your toxic relationship, but also obsessed with it. These feelings keep you isolated.	5. You have a Mental Health Village that doesn't judge you and supports your emotional recovery. You have a more fun and full life than before.
6. You drop everything at a moment's notice to please or rescue your romantic partner and feel like you're in a one-way relationship.	6. You don't allow anyone to use you. You stop rescuing your toxic partner recognizing he has his own path to recovery.
7. You worry your romantic partner is lying to and/or cheating on you.	7. You come out of denial and don't tolerate lies and infidelity; living by the motto that "Trust is Earned, not Given."

8. You want to leave your relationship permanently, but just when you're getting strong alone, he returns and sucks you in again.	8. You maintain self-respect in the relationship or find the strength to leave for good.

These may seem like extravagant outcomes, but if you're willing to dive in and swim, these are just the tip of the iceberg.

The 12 Exercises

You can do these exercises at lightning speed or as slow as a tortoise on Sunday. There's no perfect way to work this program. *You* set the pace.

But I'd like to suggest you walk through these exercises more than once. We have layers of consciousness that we can't access in one run-through. All our hidden stumbling blocks are revealed in time, one layer at a time.

This work is likely to dredge up some painful feelings, but I'm here to tell you that it's the most important work you'll ever do.

Literary Resources

In addition to reading the timely articles on my relationship website, ShannonColleary.com – I also recommend that you consult the other emotional-health resources listed in the final chapter of this book.

I'm happy to share the resources that had the biggest impact on my recovery and my life.

Just as it "takes a village to raise a child," I believe it also takes a village to raise our mental and emotional health.

Now let's fire up our jets (okay, that was corny, but I couldn't resist) and get to work.

PART ONE:

THE PROBLEM

Spoiler Alert
It's *not* the Asshat.

NINE RED FLAGS THAT INDICATE YOU'RE DATING AN ASSHAT

If we haven't grown up with healthy relationship role models, we may not know what a healthy relationship looks like.

We may not even *realize* our relationship is toxic.

So, if you're feeling confused about whether the man you're dating is an Asshat, let me offer you some clarity.

Red Flag #1: He Came On Strong in the Beginning, then Cooled Off Fast Once You Were Hooked.

At first your guy seemed besotted and intense. He wanted intimacy and sex at hyper-speed. But after sex you felt like Teri Garr in film classic, *Tootsie*:

"After I sleep with a guy, he acts like he owes me money."

Chloe's Story

Chloe, a recent client, had a history of dating men who criticized, lied and cheated on her. But when Jim suggested they get together for coffee she was excited.

Since she'd met him in her church group, Chloe figured Jim was a safe bet.

She felt like she knew him well, based on social interactions and talks he'd given at church, plus he was so enthusiastic about her.

On their very first date, they slept together. By the end of the first week Jim told Chloe she was "the woman he'd been looking for his whole life."

He'd even asked her to come home with him for the holidays to meet his family and had indicated he might want to *live* with her someday.

Chloe felt a little uncomfortable with the blistering pace Jim set. But she also yearned to be *wanted*.

Tossing her hesitation aside, Chloe dove in. Their infatuation period lasted one month. Right up until Chloe told Jim she'd purchased airline tickets to meet his family like he'd wanted.

Jim fled the scene as if the Zombie Apocalypse were coming. He told Chloe it was because she loved him more than he loved her.

You can imagine how mind-boggling this was, considering how intense Jim had been at the beginning of the relationship.

Katie's Story

Katie met Aaron at a work party. He was a friend of one of her co-workers. She thought he was cute, but balked when he pressed for a date.

Katie had recently clawed her way out of a six-year relationship with an Asshat extraordinaire and didn't think she was ready to date yet.

Aaron assured her he was "just talking about dinner and a movie."

Katie thought, "Well, what the hell?" It beat a night home alone with a vat of Haagen Daz and "Dancing with the Stars."

"Dinner and a movie" went perfectly well. Aaron was polite and gave Katie a brotherly hug goodnight on her door stoop.

He called the next morning invited her to the beach for the following weekend.

Again, Katie wasn't particularly keen, but didn't have any real reason *not* to go. Besides, her bruised and battered ego was soaking up the attention.

As Aaron drove Katie home after a pleasant day of sun, surf and sand, he asked if she'd mind stopping by his house because he had a "little surprise" for her.

Katie hesitated. It was only the second date. But Aaron's roommate was the co-worker who'd introduced them, so Katie figured Aaron wasn't a bloodthirsty psychopath.

Once they arrived and had greeted the roommate, Aaron whisked Katie into his bedroom then asked if he could blindfold her.

Wait, what?

"Don't worry," Aaron assured Katie. "You can take the blindfold off any time, just let me slip it on you for a moment."

Katie shrugged. *Why not?* She heard Aaron exit, then re-enter the room. She felt his bed sink a little as he sat down next to her.

"Now, open your mouth," he instructed.

"Open my *mouth*?"

"I promise I won't put anything in your mouth you won't like."

Okaaaay. Katie certainly had to admire Aaron's nerve. She opened her mouth and Aaron put something delicious inside.

Katie chewed. "It's a strawberry."

"Correct," Aaron affirmed.

Maybe he was more interesting than she first thought?

Next Aaron popped a piece of tangerine into Katie's mouth. Then a marshmallow. Then a piece of banana.

Ice Cream Is the Way to My Vagina!

Aaron became more delicious with each, and every bite.

They ended up in bed.

Katie skulked out of Aaron's apartment three hours later with her knickers tucked discreetly in her purse and the word "tramp" emblazoned on the inside of her brain.

Even so, Katie considered Aaron a pleasant interlude, not a man she had interest in pursuing meaningfully.

And she suspected the feeling was mutual.

Imagine her surprise when he called the next day and proclaimed that he'd decided to put all other women on a back burner.

For *her* he was thinking, quite possibly, of just "Three. Little. Words."

Three little words? He couldn't possibly mean, "I love you." Could he?

Katie thought it was weird for a man she hardly knew to make this unnecessary proclamation.

The next time Katie saw Aaron they had sex again. Even though Katie remained ambivalent about Aaron she suggested they meet the following weekend.

"That long?" Aaron moaned, like a love-struck boy.

The following weekend he called Katie just prior to their date to tell her he couldn't make it because an "emergency" had come up.

(What is it with all these emergencies?)

He wasn't "at liberty" to discuss it, but wanted her to know that while he was dealing with it, he'd be thinking those "three little words."

Was this guy serious? And, if so, what the heck was wrong with him? (Hint: The three little words turned out to be "I'm an Asshat!")

Katie decided the next time Aaron called she was going to tell him that he was rushing things and she wasn't interested in diving into a committed relationship.

She needn't have worried because Katie never saw Aaron again. He didn't pick up her calls or answer her texts. Eventually Katie just quit trying to contact him.

Are you wondering if Aaron died in a fiery collision on Pacific Coast Highway with Charlie Sheen (still living at press time)? Well, don't.

His roommate let Katie know Aaron was indeed alive and apologized for not warning her sooner that once his roommate slept with a woman he freaked out and bailed.

The good news for Katie was that she hadn't invested her heart in Aaron. He came on way too strong, way too soon.

But she still shakes her head and wonders about how long Aaron's trail of broken hearts must be.

<u>Red Flag #1 Takeaway</u>

Beware a lover that comes on strong in the beginning and cools off fast once you're hooked. Chances are, for him, love is a drug he wants to ingest to feel euphoric.

But once reality sets in – the day-to-day ordinariness of living – and he can't keep getting that same high, he'll be off to find a new person to sniff, snort or inhale.

<u>Red Flag #2</u>: He's Unreliable and Inconsistent.

Everybody can have a bad day, but unreliability is an important red flag that usually pops up in the early stages of a relationship. So, it's a good idea to pay attention before you fall into the Lothario's thrall.

If you've ignored his unreliability, you may indeed end up in some facsimile of a relationship with your guy and that's when his consistent inconsistency kicks in.

Inconsistency indicates he's conflicted.

He wants to be a functional human in an emotionally healthy relationship, but he's doing battle with the part of himself that's damaged. And the two sides are constantly at war.

"Inconsistency is a form of abuse." -- Dr. Victor Morton Ph.D.

My ex, Mister C.H., became an emotional pendulum in our five-year relationship. If I was present and wanted to connect, he'd swing away from me.

If I pulled back as a self-protective measure, he'd run to me, swearing he was a "changed man" who was ready to have the relationship I wanted.

Elated, I'd run straight back into his arms, thus beginning a "honeymoon" stage where we *seemed* to want the same things: commitment, monogamy and one day, marriage and a family.

Sometimes this "Honeymoon" stage lasted a whole week. But other times it lasted no more than an hour.

Then he'd swing away from me again. Or perhaps, in the vernacular of my favorite movie, *The Royal Tenenbaums*, he'd "shag ass."

Because of your man's two warring sides, you may find yourself constantly trying to "figure him out" hoping you can behave in a way that will get him to be more reliable and consistent.

You're fighting a losing battle. Your man can't control or even *understand* the rollercoaster of his own emotions, so how can *you* possibly do it?

When a man can't follow through on the simplest commitments that's a red flag that he'll never come through on bigger commitments; like marriage, finances and caring for children.

Red Flag #3: He Warns You He's an Asshat.

Please believe him!!!

There are plenty of early red flags your heartbreaker doesn't want you to notice, but here's the funny thing about people: they *always* tell you who they are, and they often tell you right away.

My Story

Prior to recovering from my addiction to rakes and rapscallions, I too had been warned. The very first time I met Mister C.H. he showed his hand.

We met at a friends' house where he pursued me like the wolf does Vince Vaughn's "little bunny rabbit," extracting my phone number the way an NSA spy extracts national secrets from Vladimir Putin's mistress.

(Boy, the analogies are zooming by like twin Cessnas!)

I was flattered. Until a loyal friend informed me that the moment I left the party, Mister C.H. got a *second* woman's phone number using the same approach.

I let it slide. After all, we'd just met. Why *shouldn't* he pursue more than one lady at a time?

Also, his gorgeous, thick, curly black hair and set of roguish dimples blinded my sanity. Put him in his policeman's uniform and I was a goner.

Bye-bye little red flag.

Three weeks into our courtship Mister C.H. arrived unexpectedly at a party I'd gone to solo. He pulled me outside and told me how much he desired me.

"You have so much energy that I just want to suck it all out of you!" he said, his eyes boring into my very soul.

He stood right there and told me he was going to be an emotional vampire.

And guess what? I invited him in.

For the next five years, he sucked up all my jet fuel.

Let Me In!
I Promise You
Won't Feel a
Thing!

The Frenchman

My client Helen was newly single after a long, dissatisfying relationship, when she developed a mad crush on a gorgeous, exotic Frenchman.

Friends warned her that the Frenchman was a Lothario, going through women the way victims of Avian flu go through Kleenex.

Helen decided she didn't care. She just "wanted to have fun," and didn't need a sexual liaison with a hot Frenchman to turn into anything serious.

She'd count it as a pre-marital adventure to think back on fondly.

Cut To: A Party at a Mutual Friend's House.

The Frenchman was there. Helen was there. "Seducing the Frenchman" was her mission, should she choose to accept it.

Helen spent the evening chatting up Francois (admittedly not his name), getting him drinks and finally offering to give him a ride home when he was too drunk to drive.

(Also not a promising sign.)

When Helen pulled up to the curb in front of the Frenchman's apartment, she gazed at him in a way she hoped was seductive.

But instead of inviting her in, Francois looked Helen blearily in the eye and growled, "What do you want from me?"

Helen was taken aback. "Um," she mumbled, "Nothing?"

"You don't want *anything* from me?" Francois queried, his eyes narrowing into suspicious slits.

Helen considered admitting she wanted a tawdry roll in the hay, but was too embarrassed. "No, I don't want anything from you."

"Good. Because I've got *nothing* to give. So ... you want to come inside?"

Francois told Helen right there, flat out. *He had nothing to give!* Which was admirable when you think about it

Later, in The Solution, I'll tell you how Helen responded, but for now it pays to remember:

Toxic People <u>Know</u> They're Toxic and Will Often Warn You Right Away!

<u>Red Flag #4</u>: He Never Wants to Meet Your Friends or Family.

Once the honeymoon stage is over and the intense sexual bonding is complete, you may find it almost impossible to get your man to meet the people you care about.

Maybe he says he wants to "take thing slow" or is "socially shy" or "too tired, too over-worked, too stressed out, too ..."

Well. You get the picture.

The truth is, in the words of self-help author Greg Behrendt, "He's just not that into you."

Or he may be incapable of committed love. Or maybe he *is* in love with you, but knows he's damaged and is going to screw things up and break your heart.

He senses that your friends and family will see him for the heart-breaker he is.

During this phase of your relationship (which could last a very long time, depending on your tolerance level) you're most likely to see your man when he just *happens* to be in the neighborhood and drops by for a booty call.

Or wants you to do his laundry. Or lend him money – but I digress.

He might also come around when you've finally had enough of his shenanigans and retreat. There's nothing more attractive to a Lothario than a woman who *doesn't* want him.

He'll do *anything* you want, including making plans with your loved ones, until he has you back.

Then his resistance rears its ugly head again, but *this time* it's even stronger. And you've become weaker and less insistent because you're most likely addicted to your Romeo.

When We're Addicted to Someone We Become Entrenched in an Emotional Cycle of Abuse.

Red Flag #5: He *Does* Attend a Family/Friend Event, But Only as a Grumpy Mute.

He won't talk. Or smile. Or engage in conversation. Your friends and family make valiant efforts to draw him out. But he does only the bare minimum to avoid seeming like an outright sociopath.

Over the course of five years, I *did* manage to coerce Mister C.H. into attending various friend and family functions but often wished I hadn't.

Sometimes he'd speak to my loved ones like a man who cared about me, filling me with hope that we'd finally jumped a hurdle.

But the very next time he'd withdraw completely. (Inconsistency! Red Flag #2) Who knows why?? It took a long time before I understood the even *he* didn't know why.

I'm Here, Aren't I? You Never Said I Had to Talk ...

Alicia's Story

My client Alicia had a social engagement that was an absolute nightmare. She'd been invited to dinner with a colleague and her husband.

Alicia asked her boyfriend Randy to come, despite the fact their relationship was a struggle. He didn't want to go so Alicia did everything but commit Hari-Kari to get him there.

She just wanted to be "normal" and avoid the appearance of being a sad singleton in front of her colleague.

The event was a disaster.

While the other three tried to engage in conversation, Randy watched a football game on the television over the bar. For the entire evening he was The Black Hole of Calcutta, uttering not one word.

Alicia was furious. She was finally ready to give Randy the heave ho. *But, wait!*

As soon as Randy sensed her sea change he appeared at Alicia's job bearing flowers, balloons and a heartbroken countenance. *He was going to change!*

In fact, he *had* changed and could now give Alicia *everything* she ever wanted. It wasn't long before she was back on the Asshat roller coaster once more.

Red Flag #6: Your Loved Ones *Really* Dislike and/or Hate Your Guy.

This might be one of those times your family is right!

Patrice's Story

None of Patrice's friends or family could *stand* her new boyfriend Eric. The few times they'd met him he was sullen and withdrawn.

Plus, they'd already heard Patrice vent one too many times about his inconsistent, unreliable Asshattery.

But there was one family member who absolutely lost her *mind* when she first met Eric. It happened over the Christmas holidays.

Patrice planned to take Eric to her sister's house for Christmas Eve so Eric could meet her family for the first time.

Eric spent the prior week coming up with an inexplicable mélange of excuses *not* to attend, but Patrice somehow managed to drug, rope and tie him up to get him there.

When they arrived, Patrice's sister opened the door hoisting her one-year-old daughter, Olivia, on her hip.

The child took one look at Eric, threw her head back and shrieked like she'd just seen Voldemort.

Patrice's sister whisked the baby away, explaining that Olivia was probably just tired and needed her nap.

Moments later Patrice's sister re-emerged with Olivia in her arms, reporting that the toddler wasn't tired after all.

But before she could finish her sentence Olivia saw Eric and shrieked in terror.

Eventually Patrice and Eric had to exit stage left because Olivia simply couldn't be in the same room with him without falling apart.

Was Olivia able to sense Eric's inner-Asshat where Patrice was sex-and-love blind? Well, you know what they say about kids and dogs!

This incident might've been a fluke. But if you discover that the people who love you don't like your guy, I'd suggest you pay attention.

They're not sexually connected to him the way you are, hence see him without orgasm-colored glasses.

Red Flag #7: He Uses the "C" Word.

Not *that* "C" word. No, the word I'm referring to is Criticism.

My Cellulite

I fell in love with the Greek God my freshman year of college. He was a water polo champion, sporting the aforementioned, "steel-hewn thighs."

He had one percent body fat and was my first lover. It was True Love in spades.

We had a glorious one-month period of infatuation, which seemed to taper off after I lost my virginity to him.

Shortly thereafter the C-word (criticism) made its first appearance.

We were sitting on my dorm bed. He reached over, pinched my thigh, and a few little dimples appeared. "Oh man, you've got cellulite," he exclaimed.

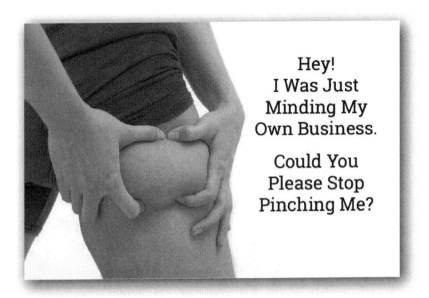

Hey!
I Was Just
Minding My
Own Business.

Could You
Please Stop
Pinching Me?

I was 19-years-old, five-foot six and weighed in at 115 pounds dripping wet.

I'd spent puberty and beyond pretty much skin-and-bones, just *wishing* I could put on a few pounds to fill out my Jordache jeans. So, cellulite was, as yet, unknown to me.

Until the Greek God informed me that cellulite:

* Is disgusting and verges on sinful. (Even though 9 out of 10 women have it.)
* Is caused by laziness and lack of discipline.
* Makes men not want to have sex with you.
* I'd never be good enough until my thighs looked and felt as steel-hewn as his.

My response to this was to stop wearing shorts and skirts and to drape cover-ups over my bathing suit. But the criticism didn't stop there.

* My hair looked like a wig from the movie *Gremlins*.
* My chin was bigger than Jay Leno's.

* And my lady bits could double for a Yeti. (I hadn't learned about trimming yet.)

While sometimes these comments were made in jest, ultimately they were meant to keep me in my place.

By making me feel smaller and smaller, the Greek God ensured I felt unentitled to my wants and even my needs in the relationship.

I began to believe that, considering all my many flaws, I was lucky to get him and deserved the times he treated me poorly.

Jenna's Story

Asshats will even criticize us for reacting negatively to their outrageous behavior.

My client Jenna was living with Matt, her boyfriend of three years. He'd been inconsistent and unreliable throughout their relationship.

When they moved in together, Jenna thought that volatility would end. But Matt's bad behavior ramped up exponentially.

He began getting home from work several hours later than expected and wouldn't answer Jenna's texts or phone calls.

One night, at 4 a.m., Matt *still* wasn't home from "work" and remained incommunicado.

In desperation, Jenna called one of Matt's colleagues, waking him up.

He told Jenna that he'd been out with Matt at a bar earlier, but that they'd parted ways at midnight.

Jenna spent the night imagining all the low-down, unfaithful shenanigans Matt was most likely up to.

By the time he finally returned home at 7 a.m. Jenna was a sleepless, infuriated banshee. Yet he somehow managed to steal her thunder.

"Did you call Colin at four in the morning?" he yelled.

"Yes, I was looking for you and you wouldn't answer your phone!"

Matt rolled his eyes in disgust. "That's incredibly embarrassing," he informed Jenna. "You're acting like white trash."

Oh, yes he did!

And Jenna -- who'd grown up in a home filled with inconsistency and infidelity -- and who was afflicted with low self-esteem because of it, felt ashamed for embarrassing Matt by acting like "white trash."

Criticism Makes Us Believe We're the Ones Who Are Damaged, Not Our Abusers.

Red Flag #8: He Tells You You're Paranoid When You See Signs He's Cheating.

Just hearing the phrase, "You're paranoid," ought to be a little red flag.

Molly's Story

After two years of haranguing, prodding and cajoling, Molly managed to extract an apartment key from her boyfriend Willem.

She was thrilled. She felt certain the key was a sign she and Will were entering a new era of closeness and commitment.

They had to be, right?

Or Will wouldn't have given her a key to his apartment where she could let herself in any time of the day or night!

Finally, she could relax and know that she was his Only One.

Two months later ... Willem wanted his key back!

Molly was shocked. She thought they'd reached a milestone and now, suddenly, they were going backwards?

To Molly that meant three possibilities:

Redhead, Brunette or Blonde

Perhaps, like Molly, you feel uneasy about what happens in your man's life when you're not around. Maybe you've noticed behavior that indicates infidelity.

A few examples:

*   He doesn't want you to see who he's texting.
*   He's uber-territorial about his computer.
*   He doesn't want you just 'dropping by' without calling first.
*   He accuses you of snooping when you're looking for the stapler on his desk.
*   He cancels plans at the last minute for no good reason.
*   He's defensive and angry when you ask about his schedule.
*   He has a new "friendship" with someone of the opposite sex that you haven't met.
*   He acts like a dead fish in bed.

Finally, you muster the courage to ask him what's wrong. *Is he seeing someone else?*

This is when he goes on the offensive. Suddenly you're "too needy," "too clingy," "smothering him," "paranoid," "need to get a life."

He's right. You *do* need to get a life. One without him!

Beware a Love Who Attacks You for Not Trusting Him, Rather Than Demonstrating His Trustworthiness.

Caveat: If *all* the people you date think you're too needy, clingy or smother-y, you *might* be. Counseling can help you determine why you can't trust people when there's no evidence to the contrary.

Red Flag #9: He Cheats on You.

This isn't a red flag. It's an anvil dropping on your head.

- * He secretly cheats on you.
- * He overtly cheats on you.
- * He cheats on you in a box, with a fox, wearing socks.

Then He Makes You Feel Bad for Leaving Him Because He Cheated!

I'll set the stage: you suspected something might be going on, but *now* you have proof!

You discovered another woman's lacy G-string in your bed and your man has confessed he slept with the dog walker while you were across the country helping your mom during her chemotherapy.

Now you must figure out whether you're going to take your man back.

Because he's *already* pleading for your forgiveness and swearing you'll never find another woman's G-string in your bed again.

He doesn't know what he'll do without you, except perish.

Due to your own childhood-induced:

- * **Overabundance of empathy and ...**
- * **Misplaced sense of responsibility**

… you immediately find justifications for his hurtful behavior and reasons to take him back. In no particular order the reasons are:

1. He Had a Terrible Childhood

When he was little his mom left the family for a younger man named Raoul. They were last seen in a mini-mall in Arcadia with their new kids (or some similar sob story).

So of *course* your man has issues with attachment!

If you can just love him for who he is and promise you'll never leave him like his mother did, you can heal his psychic wounds and the cheating will stop. (This is what they call "Stinking Thinking" In Twelve Step recovery.)

2. You Should've Been Sexier

That's it! *You're* the problem!

You aren't thin enough, full-figured enough, your boobs are too small, too big, your fanny too round, too flat, you have no waist, you're long-waisted.

But, hello? Was Halle Berry not sexy enough to keep her men faithful? Jennifer Aniston? Reese Witherspoon? Gwen Stefani? I think you get my point.

If a man is a serial cheater, *he's* to blame.

3. He Only Cheated Because You're Too Clingy

Now we're on to something! He convinces you that your neurotic clinginess didn't come about *because* he cheated, but that he cheated *because* of your neurotic clinginess!

4. You Put Too Much Pressure on Him

You should *never* have told him that you wanted marriage and kids and the white picket fence. Or a key to his apartment. Or even a drawer.

Even though he *says* he wants those things too, "just not right now."

So maybe if you stop pressuring him, eventually you'll be around sooooo long he'll marry you and make all your dreams come true.

Stop and ask yourself, do you really want to marry someone who has to be leveraged, hornswoggled, finagled and duped into marrying you? Of course you don't.

Because, my fellow Recovery Road-Warrior, you are far too valuable to have to beg. With your vast supply of Love, Empathy and Compassion you're a catch for a good man!

So, it's time to start building your self-esteem. I'll help you do that in The Solution.

TEN CHARACTER TRAITS IN PARTNERS OF ASSHATS

This chapter is all about *you* and the reasons you might be susceptible to scoundrels and the emotional cycle of abuse.

By learning about, uncovering and working on these traits you can finally feel the peace of "emotional sobriety." Emotional sobriety allows you to:

Stop Controlling Your Guy, Gain Control of Your Life and Invite Real Love.

Emotional sobriety isn't about feeling great. It means coming out of denial about our circumstances and ourselves. It's about getting real.

Psychotherapist Ingrid Mathieu, Ph.D. writes this:

"People in [emotional and mental] recovery want the ability to access all of their feelings, because being present to what is real is what enables choices, and choices propel people towards their most authentic and fulfilling *sober* life."

So let's start moving out of denial by unearthing the character traits in partners of Asshats.

Trait #1: Your Family of Origin Was Toxic

There's dysfunction in *every* family. We're all human and we all make mistakes.

But there are *degrees* of dysfunction that can have far-reaching impact. That's the arena we're focusing on here.

I come from a long line of women (and men) who were emotionally abused and/or neglected by Asshats.

My paternal grandfather had a gambling addiction. This compelled my dad to start working by age seven. He hid his earnings under his bed where his father wouldn't find them.

My paternal grandmother was an angry, negative woman who frequently berated and criticized her gambling husband because of her deep disappointment in him and in life.

As a result, my dad has struggled with being critical, negative and never feeling financially secure enough.

Meanwhile, my maternal grandmother was married to a dyed-in-the-wool skirt-chaser who'd be married a total of seven times before he took his last breath.

And then there's my stepfather, Trent.

Trent spent much of his marriage to my mom lying, cheating and just generally being a moody bastard who got mad at her for being mad at him when he behaved like an Asshat.

(He was also a Hot Cop. Calling Dr. Freud!)

By the time I came of dating age I'd witnessed or experienced inconsistency, neglect, lying, cheating, criticism and disrespect.

Because these behaviors were familiar to me, being with Asshats felt like "home." It was difficult for me to skip the heartbreakers and invite Real Love.

Destructive Relationships Can Feel "Right" Because They're Familiar.

If you come from generations of dysfunction, you may not be able to determine what behavior is acceptable.

You might idealize True Love as an escape from your crazy past only to find yourself in equal chaos. And the cycle of dysfunction goes on.

Trait #2: You Have an Intense Need for Love and Affection

Are you a person who has a difficult time *not* being in a romantic relationship? Then you might have "an intense need for love and affection."

Penny's Story

From the moment Penny hit puberty she was *always* in some kind of romantic entanglement.

Her brief moments of single-dom left Penny feeling restless and bored. She didn't feel alive unless a man was pursuing her.

Penny's favorite state-of-being was the "falling in love" stage at the beginning of a relationship, when the sex was most red-hot.

Huge butterflies flapped around in her stomach and she yearned to be with her man every second, as if they were tragically doomed lovers separated by war.

To Penny that was the very definition of LOVE!

"People who've been emotionally used and/or neglected as children, are most at risk for love addiction." -- Sex & Love Addiction/Recovery Ranch

Penny's parents were in a destructive relationship punctuated by threats of divorce, mutual infidelity and abuse of drugs and alcohol.

Her role was to provide her parents with advice, support, mediation and lots of smoke and mirrors.

She hid her mother's prescription drugs from her dad, and told her mom it was a "wrong number" when women called for her father.

This set Penny up for many years of pursuing unpredictable, emotionally unavailable men whom she tried to control through caretaking, rescuing and sex.

Robert Weiss of *The Centers for Relationship and Sexual Recovery at The Ranch* offers these signs of Love Addiction:

1. Endlessly searching for *The One.*
2. Attracting troubled, addicted, abusive or emotionally unavailable partners.
3. Mistaking sex and romance for intimate love.
4. Using sex and/or love to mask loneliness or unhappiness.
5. Using seduction, sex or other schemes to attract or hold onto a partner.
6. Dressing seductively to attract attention, take risks or feel empowered.
7. Crossing sexual and relationship boundaries. (For instance: taking your boss to bed.)
8. Repeatedly "falling in love" with strangers.

Love at First Sight

Let me say a word about Penny's favorite bugaboo, Love at First Sight.

LAFS has nothing to do with compatibility, true intimacy, committed love or even your eyes! *LAFS* is our genitals talking.

It's our damaged inner child attempting to heal her pain by revisiting the same chaos, abandonment, neglect and emotional abuse she experienced in childhood.

Trait #3: You Struggle With Low Self-Esteem

And honestly, who doesn't from time to time? But you don't want low self-esteem to keep you stuck in painful circumstances.

Rosemary's Story

My client Rosemary didn't worry much about her self-esteem. She was feeling pretty fly because a prestigious brokerage firm had offered her a management job straight out of her Ivy League college.

Then she met her Asshat.

Trevor was gorgeous, a little wild and a lot hot. Rosemary became sexually intimate with him right away.

But once Trevor knew he'd reeled her in, the emotional abuse began. Their emotional abuse cycle looked something like this:

* Rosemary gave and gave -- sexually, emotionally, financially -- to get closer to Trevor, wanting more of a commitment.
* In response, Trevor became moody, critical, inconsistent and secretive.
* So, Rosemary gave more to control his behavior.
* *Not gonna happen!* Trevor's moodiness, criticism, inconsistency and sneakiness increased.
* *What the hell?* Rosemary threatened to leave.
* Trevor shrugged. (He'd heard it before.)
* As God was her witness, Rosemary *did* leave!
* For five seconds Rosemary felt good about her decision.
* Then she freaked out. *Maybe if she'd just given Trevor a little bit more, he'd treat her better?*
* Like a dog with her tail between her legs, Rosemary returned.
* Rosemary might find out Trevor cheated on her while she was away.

* Trevor insisted it was her fault for leaving. Didn't she understand?
* Of course she did.

Rosemary had a lot of rock bottom moments that included the 3 a.m. stakeouts previously mentioned. In the middle of it all, Rosemary would think:

How did this happen to me?? I was voted "Girl Who Contributed the Most to her School!"

It turns out that Rosemary spent much of her childhood trying to get her busy, distant, critical dad's approval.

She brought good grades to him, "like a dog fetching a newspaper and waiting to be patted on the head."

She competed with siblings for her dad's attention, bragged and exaggerated to impress him, and soared or sank depending on how he gave or withheld praise.

Dr. Marilyn J. Sorensen of *The Self-Esteem Institute* has this to say about low self-esteem sufferers:

"Desperately seeking reassurance that they are lovable, those with low self-esteem look outside themselves and at the behavior of those closest to them to find answers to the question of being lovable."

She goes on to say that if they don't get the love and approval they seek, these sufferers will:

* Try harder to please to win the love and attention of the significant other.

* Become angry when they feel the significant other is withholding what they need.
* Feel they must be deserving of this treatment and conclude that they are indeed unlovable.

In the midst of Rosemary's hellish relationship, she knew she had to build her self-esteem if she was ever going to break away from her ne'er-do-well.

A Quick Note About Low Self-Esteem & Rebellion

Some of us with low self-esteem do the *exact opposite* of looking outside ourselves for approval.

Some of us rebel against those whose approval we secretly, desperately want. It's our attempt to stop caring about what they think of us, or our bid for attention, even if it's negative attention

Unfortunately, both people-pleasing and rebelling are about someone else. Neither aids us in our journey to self-esteem.

Trait #4: You Don't Set Healthy Boundaries

First, what do I mean when I use the vaguely crunchy-granola phrase "healthy boundaries?" I mean exactly this:

Protecting those aspects of your life that no healthy partner would threaten: your body, your family relationships and responsibilities, your money, safety and security.

Here are some specific examples of "setting healthy boundaries" to protect yourself:

* You won't accept sex when what you want is Real Love.
* You won't abandon plans with others you love when your "boyfriend" wants a booty call after he hasn't talked to you in over a month.

* You won't lend your man your paycheck for the fiftieth time as your landlord is evicting you.
* You won't … well, I think you get my point.

When we undertake the task of squeezing Real Love out of an Asshat, our healthy boundaries can fall by the wayside.

We can spend years twisting ourselves into different pretzel shapes, often abandoning ourselves, and our principles to keep this kind of partner engaged.

Sandy's Story

Sandy and her beau Jeremy had been dating for almost four years. During that time he admitted he was a sex addict.

Each time Sandy caught him cheating, Jeremy tearfully promised to get help. So Sandy stayed. But within weeks he'd be back in business.

Because Sandy kept failing to leave the relationship, she decided, "If you can't beat 'em, join 'em."

She agreed to participate in a ménage à trois with a second woman, despite the fact doing so made her incredibly uncomfortable.

In the midst of the tryst Sandy bolted. She recognized she'd hit rock bottom.

Trait #5: You Are Codependent

Melody Beattie, author of the seminal book *Codependent No More: How to Stop Controlling Others and Start Caring for Yourself*, defines a codependent person this way:

"One who has let another person's behavior affect him or her, and who is obsessed with controlling that person's behavior."

Beattie throws a wide net. She writes that the "other person" might be a child, an adult, a spouse, basically anyone we want to control.

For our purposes, we're focusing on the Asshat.

Twelve Step Recovery

In The Solution I'm going to go into detail about how Twelve Step programs were pivotal in my recovery journey, but until then I highly recommend you read the Twelve Step book *Codependents Anonymous (CODA)*, which defines codependence like this:

> "Codependence is a disease that deteriorates our souls. It affects our personal lives; our families, children, friends, and relatives; our businesses and careers; or our health; and our spiritual growth.
>
> "It is debilitating and, if left untreated, causes us to become more destructive to ourselves, and others. Many of us come to a point when we must look beyond ourselves for help."

There are two cool things imbedded in that definition. The first alleviates our **Shame** and the second offers **Hope.**

Here's what I mean:

1. "Codependence is a disease."

Many of us are painfully ashamed of our self-destructive relationship with an Asshat. (We might even be lying to friends and family about our situation.)

But if we can embrace codependence as a *"disease,"* we can boot Shame.

Would we be ashamed of ourselves if we had a disease like cancer? Or Lupus? No? Then we mustn't be ashamed of ourselves if we're afflicted with codependence.

2. "Many of us come to a point when we must look beyond ourselves for help."

This gives us Hope that we don't have to recover from the disease of codependence and the cycle-of-futility all by ourselves. Help is available – it's waiting.

CODA is referring to the Twelve Step recovery groups as a source "beyond ourselves" that we can reach out to.

I'll get into Twelve Step concepts in The Solution. Atheists and agnostics fear not, this can be helpful for you too.

<u>Trait #6</u>: Your Behavior Is Crazier Than the Asshat!

There were many times I out-crazied both my exes.

Sure they were inconsistent, unreliable, critical and unfaithful. But I yelled, screamed, jumped up and down, slapped them (each once), threw stuff at their heads and ran down the street after their cars.

Can we say BONKERS?!!!!

I believe my insanity stemmed from my codependency. Melody Beattie has the best explanation for my craziness. She writes:

"We feel crazy because we are lying to ourselves. We feel crazy because we are believing other people's lies.

"Nothing will help us feel crazy faster than being lied to. Believing lies disrupts the core of our being.

"The deep instinctive part of us that knows the truth, but we are pushing that part away and telling it, 'You're wrong, shut up.'

"We decide there's something fundamentally wrong with us for being suspicious and we label ourselves, and our inner-most, intuitive being as untrustworthy."

So yes, when you *feel* crazy, you *act* crazy. And I'm just glad most of my behavior pre-dates Snap Chat!

Trait #7: You Have a God Complex

Some of us obtained our sense of security and positive self-image from rescuing and/or caretaking our dysfunctional parents.

Being "wise" children was a point of pride and set us up to repeat those patterns to detrimental effect in adulthood.

In short, we often play God by caretaking our Asshat, whether he wants us to or not.

And let me be clear, "care*taking*" has nothing to do with its healthy counterpart, "care*giving*."

A Brief Comparison

Recovery site *Expressing Counseling and Coaching* has this to say:

"Care*taking* is … rooted in insecurity and a need to be in control. Care*giving* is an expression of kindness and love."

So, if you spend your time advising, fixing and rescuing your rapscallion, chances are you're care*taking*, rather than care*giving*.

You're crossing your lover's boundaries and telling him how to behave and live his life.

* A care*taker* becomes a mother, doctor, priest, psychologist and nag, manipulating the Asshat to behave in ways that would make her happier.
* A care*giver* allows people the dignity of making their own decisions.
* A care*taker* gives and gives until she's physically, spiritually, emotionally and even financially drained and has nothing left to give.
* A care*giver* knows she must take care of herself first to be any good to anyone else.
* A care*taker* often ends up filled with repressed anger and resentment, feeling unappreciated for all the work she does on her man's behalf.

Then guess what kicks in?

Trait # 8: You Have a Martyr Complex

After all that "selfless" giving and giving, we want something in return, dammit! So, we become whiners and victims, griping and moaning until even we can hardly stand ourselves.

If you find yourself constantly people-pleasing, caretaking and rescuing your man, followed by bitching, moaning, complaining and resentment, ask yourself this:

Is it worth it?

Are your Godlike wisdom and self-sacrificing martyr image really worth the burnout that's sure to follow?

Do you want to be in or try to control a relationship where you never have your own needs filled? And you secretly become a seething pit of rage that eventually blows up, incinerating all before it?

I don't think so! (More on how to remedy this in The Solution.)

Trait #9: You Believe Things Will Change if You Just Try Harder.

Let's set the scene, shall we?

You're madly infatuated with a stud-muffin we'll call Val. He's sexy and gorgeous and you're as whipped as Hera was by that philanderer Zeus.

But being with Val, while exciting, is also *incredibly* frustrating. He's often unreliable, not calling when he says he will, showing up late for dates, if at all.

His moods are unpredictable. Sometimes he wants to bend you over in aisle 13 at Wal-Mart; other times he finds you utterly undesirable. You think things like this:

He'd be loving, consistent and want me all the time if I were prettier, smarter, more independent, less needy, more perky, less available, more understanding, less demanding.

And the beat goes on.

So, you try *harder*. You wear more make-up, get a new hairstyle, never say "no" in bed. You listen to all his problems and, of course, try to fix them. But none of it works. So, you continue thinking you can fix it by doing *even more*.

My colleague Dr. Gary Penn Ph.D. typifies this mindset as "very young thinking." He says:

"When I'm five or six-years-old and my mom is neglectful or angry or unavailable, I think I must be a bad boy. I take ownership. I don't have the wherewithal at that age to realize that maybe it's not about me.

"Maybe my mother is out of control or has her own painful history and trauma. I can't determine who's at fault so I automatically go to, *'What did I do?'*"

Dr. Penn asks his clients how often they've blamed themselves when someone else has treated them poorly. Do they think:

"What did *I* do to make you talk to me this way, to treat me this way?"

Instead of thinking:

"You really want to hurt me. You really want to make me feel bad about myself. And that's on you, not me."

Granted, there *are* times we screw up and need to try harder to improve our relationships.

But, if we find that our romantic partner continues to treat us badly as we peel him grapes and fan him with the wings of a thousand angels, we're falling into the trap that "trying harder" will fix things.

It won't work. And I'll tell you why.

I want you to memorize this, write it on your bathroom mirror in lipstick, tattoo it on your biceps, brand it on your rear end, because it may be the most important concept you take away from this section of the book.

"The 3 Cs of Acceptance" -- You Didn't <u>Cause</u> the Asshat's Dysfunction. You Can't <u>Control</u> It. And You Can't <u>Cure</u> It.

<u>Trait #10:</u> You're Stuck in Break Up/Make Up Cycles.

My compatriot, I've been there. I don't have enough fingers and toes to count all the times I flounced off in a huff, only to come groveling back and ask for more mistreatment.

"That's it, you Asshole! I've had it! I *never* want to see you again as long as cockroaches live!" I'd yell.

Followed in approximately sixty minutes by my groveling return, "Perhaps I was a bit hasty. Can you let me in so you can continue to treat me like crap? I even brought your favorite Fiery Doritos Taco Supreme from Taco Bell!"

Every time we make threats we're incapable of carrying out, our self-esteem and self-love take a massive nosedive.

Having these 10 character traits doesn't mean you suck. It just means you'll need a little elbow grease to vanquish them in The Solution.

YOUR BRAIN ON SEX: FOUR REASONS YOU STAY WHEN YOU SHOULD GO

Sex needs its own chapter because it actually trumps all. It tricks you into ignoring the red flags and single-handedly feeds our codependent character traits.

Sex is the most powerful tool an Asshat can use to keep us addicted to the cycle of abuse. Because sex does a number on the brain, just like any chemical-inducing drug.

Even Walter White Wasn't Dealing with Chemicals as Potent as These!

In her article, "Your Brain on Love, Sex and the Narcissist: Addiction to our Abusers," Shahida Arabi, former president of the NYU chapter of NOW (The National Organization for Women) describes the four components of sexual brain chemistry that can addict us to our emotional abuser.

1. Oxytocin

"This hormone, known famously as the 'cuddle' or 'love hormone' is released during touching, orgasm and sexual intercourse. It promotes attachment and trust. It is the same hormone released by the hypothalamus that enables bonding between mother and child."

I found sex with my two emotionally abusive boyfriends initially incendiary. Why couldn't I repeat that same dangerous, explosive sex with a "nice guy?"

Arabi has an answer:

"Charming emotional predators such as narcissists are able to mirror our deepest sexual and emotional desires, which leads to a strong sexual bond, which then, of course, releases oxytocin, and promotes even more trust and attachment.

"Meanwhile, the narcissist, who is usually devoid of empathy and does not form these types of close attachments, is able to move on to his … next source of supply without much thought or remorse."

Many of my private clients mistakenly believed that their intense sexual bonding was mutual, until the Romeo proved otherwise.

And while I've mentioned that Asshats can come in *any* gender, Arabi reports:

"The addictive nature of oxytocin is also gendered. The unfortunate fact is that estrogen promotes the effects of oxytocin bonding whereas testosterone discourages it. This makes it more difficult for females in *any type* of relationship to detach from the bond as quickly as men."

And oxytocin isn't the only culprit.

2. Dopamine

In her *Psychology Today* article, "Dopamine: Why It's So Hard to 'Just Say No,'" Samantha Smithstein Psy.D. writes:

"Both addictive drugs and highly pleasurable or intense experiences ... such as ... an orgasm, trigger the release of the brain chemical dopamine, which in turn creates a reward circuit in the brain.

"This circuit registers that intense experience as 'important' and creates lasting memories of it as a pleasurable experience.

"Dopamine changes the brain on a cellular level, commanding the brain to 'do it again,' which heightens the possibility of relapse even long after the behavior ... has stopped."

If there's any reason to approach your recovery with self-compassion rather than self-criticism *this* is it.

Arabi's research further reveals that unpredictable relationships are particularly dopamine-inducing. She writes:

"Abusive tactics like intermittent reinforcement work well with our dopamine system, because studies show that dopamine flows more readily when the rewards are given out on an unpredictable schedule rather than predictably after conditioned cues."

So, guess what? After your "honeymoon" phase releases dopamine, the Asshat's unreliability and inconsistency throw gasoline on the fire. But addiction doesn't end with the "pleasure" hormones.

3. Adrenaline

The stress hormones can be equally addictive. Arabi reports:

> "Adrenaline prepares our body for the flight-or-fight response, and [is] also a culprit in biochemical reactions to our abusers.
>
> "Adrenaline promotes an antidepressant effect triggering fear and anxiety, which then releases dopamine. This can cause us to become 'adrenaline junkies,' addicted to the rush of vacillating between *bonding* and *betrayal*."

But the piece of reportage I found most illuminating in Arabi's well-researched story was what she calls "Trauma Bonding."

4. Trauma Bonding

This particularly affects those of us who've grown up in violent or emotionally abusive homes. She writes:

> "Trauma bonding occurs after intense, emotional experiences with our abusers and tethers us to them, creating subconscious patterns of attachment that are very difficult to detach from.
>
> "It is part of the phenomenon known as Stockholm Syndrome, in which [hostages] become attached to their perpetrators and even defend their captors."

The bottom line is, we who love Asshats need to understand not just our past – which reveals why we're drawn to them – but also to why our brain chemistry keeps us in the relationship.

Understanding this moves us from self-judgment into self-compassion as we pursue recovery.

SIX WAYS LOVING A HEARTBREAKER CHANGES US

When we're in the thick of our day-to-day life with an Asshat we don't *see* the long-term negative impact our relationship has on our mood, self-esteem, self-confidence, values, goals and our other meaningful relationships.

We can transform from a motivated, healthy, happy person into a miserable, sniveling wreck no one wants to be around without even knowing it's happening.

This is reminiscent of the story of the frog who is put in a pool of cool water. He doesn't realize it's actually a pot on a stove that is slowly coming to boil. He's cooked and ready to eat before he even knows it.

And I don't think we want to turn into a delicious pair of frog legs on our toxic roustabout's silver platter.

Here are some changes in yourself you might vaguely recognize:

Change #1: Friends and Family Don't Like Who *We* Become When We're with Our Man.

It's a red flag when your family doesn't like your guy, but that reaction can cut both ways.

Have you ever had someone who really loves you, someone who *truly* has your back, say something like this to you:

"It's not that I don't like your boyfriend/lover/spouse. It's just that I don't like who *you* become when you're with him. I feel like you're not being your *true* self."

I can't tell you how many times I heard some variation of that line from friends and family while I was dating each of my heartbreakers.

But I was in denial because I was neck-deep in an Oxytocin-Dopamine Tsunami of addiction to the relationships and didn't want to look too closely at what they were costing me.

My relationship with The Greek God encompassed most of my college years. And along with the damage he did to my body image, he dinged me in other ways too.

After several months of dating, he began having questionable relationships with other women.

Consequently, I morphed from a carefree, fun-loving, popular co-ed into an isolated, loner who developed spy skills on a par with the CIA, doing those patented, codependent 3 a.m. stakeouts.

This was accompanied by digging through his personal papers and letters, driving hours to see if he was where he *said* he was, then driving back without him even knowing I'd been there.

My friends and family noticed how I transformed into a neurotic Geisha when my guy was around and a complaining harridan when he wasn't in sight.

They tried to intervene, which made me pull away from them. And once I'd marginalized the closest people in my life, I further isolated myself in the painful relationship.

Change #2: *We Become Unreliable and Inconsistent.*

When the man we love is inconsistent and unreliable, we can often mirror him, becoming unreliable and inconsistent with everyone *except* our Romeo.

For *him* we'll make ourselves available at a ping, waiting around hours, nay *days* for him to deign to see us.

But then we start being late for or cancelling appointments with friends, family and colleagues to be forever on-call for our unpredictable Asshat.

And as we wait – at the beck and call of our lover – other meaningful relationships fall by the wayside.

People stop calling because they know we'll throw them over the second our rascal crooks his little finger.

Pretty soon our lives become small, insular and lonely. And isolation is the worst thing that can happen to a relationship addict.

Change #3: We Do Weird Shit to Manage or Affirm Our Relationship.

If you live in Venice Beach, as I did, you might do things like this:

* Wear crystals to clear your chakras.
* Drift in salinized floatation tanks to calm your aura, even though you can feel the former inhabitant's long, greasy hair wrap around your arms. (I'm not kidding. Ack!)
* Stick your tongue out so your chiropractor can assess your Chi.
* Seek the wisdom of a Shaman. A Psychic. A Hypnotist. A Past-Lives Medium. Anyone who might predict a wonderful future for you and your heartbreaker, if you can *just* figure out how to control him.

Worse, you might rely on the **wrong** self-help book that affirms your choice to stay in your heart-stomping situation, with the false belief you can influence your man by applying the tools presented within!

Avoid Self-Help Books That Teach You How to Change Other People!

For a time, John Gray's still-popular *Men are From Mars, Women are From Venus* was my Bible. I'll give you an example of the absolute time wastage that occurred when I invested in using the tools in Gray's book.

In Chapter Three Gray writes:

"When a Martian (read 'man') gets upset, he never talks about what is bothering him. He would never burden another Martian with his problem unless his friend's assistance was necessary to solve the problem.

"Instead he becomes very quiet and goes to his private cave to think about his problem, mulling it over to find a solution."

Gray explains that Venusians (read 'women') need to be patient and let men come out of their cave when they're ready.

So, I waited. And waited. And waited. What I didn't realize was that:

My Man's "Cave" Was Another Woman's Vagina!

In Gray's defense, he *does* say in his introduction that his tools work best with men and women who both have goodwill toward the relationship and want to make it work.

But when you're the *only one* scratching and fighting for the relationship, Gray's advice can prolong your tolerance for very bad behavior and keep you in purgatory indefinitely.

The reality is, a relationship is only as good as the person who tries the least.

Change #4: We Turn the Narcissist's Breadcrumbs into a Rustic Loaf.

The longer we stay in a toxic circumstance, the more it depletes our jet fuel and self-worth.

Until soon we're giving the scoundrel credit for doing the *absolute minimum* to keep our relationship slogging along.

Women trapped in soul-numbing situations are extraordinary bakers. They can take their chap's breadcrumbs and whip them into a rustic loaf, because they desperately want to justify staying with him.

A Christmas Story

Caroline moved in with Toby, her boyfriend of three years, because she was certain that grappling him into a shared domicile would evolve into a marriage proposal.

Toby -- a non-commital, workaholic, traveling salesman – was emblazoned with red flags. But Caroline thought getting Toby to the altar would solve all their problems.

Toby's moping, lying, cheating and stonewalling, would disappear, as would Caroline's nagging, bitching, spying and auditioning for wife.

"Yes. Marriage is the answer! Throw in a couple of kids and we're Family of the Year!" -- Caroline

Predictably, once Caroline moved in, Toby's moping ramped up. He hedged like a hedgehog against making plans with Caroline's family and friends. And his workaholism *doubled!*

Their first Christmas together Caroline tried to harangue Toby into helping her decorate their house for the season.

She thought that if they hung tinsel, wreaths and garlands together they'd morph into a "real" couple.

Toby managed to be busy when-ever Caroline wanted to decorate.

With Christmas Eve fast approach-ing Caroline decided to decorate the tree and house alone.

She then scolded Toby for not helping her.

The next morning, she found Toby heading off for an extremely early work meeting.

Caroline rolled out of bed to start another painful, obsessive, tiny little day. Then she discovered Toby's con-tribution to their holiday home.

There on the mantel, above their fireplace, he'd hung a teeny, tiny, fig leaf sized Christmas stocking.

He'd helped her decorate!

That diminutive red stocking, with the white faux-fur trim, made Caroline's heart swell.

Sweet Jesus! He was trying! He loved her! He wanted to make her happy! Just look at that microscopic, imperceptible little boot!

Any infinitesimal gesture on Toby's part was a gem polished to a fine luster in Caroline's heart until she began to expect less and less and less, until she finally gave him credit for almost nothing at all.

I'm happy to report that Caroline pulled herself up by the Christmas bootstraps and moved out of the home she made to catch Toby.

She spent last Christmas decorating with her new roommate, Tasha, minus drama, with lots of delicious hot chocolate and mildly inedible fruitcake.

Change #5: We Become Addicted to the Cycle of Abuse.

It's important, before we move into this section, that I make it *very clear* that I'm talking about *emotional* abuse.

If you're in a physically abusive relationship put this book down right now and immediately seek help.

The National Domestic Abuse Helpline is at 1-800-799-SAFE

Here's what a classic Asshat-induced emotional cycle of abuse looks like:

1. The Asshat behaves like an Asshat. (Mopes, criticizes, lies, cheats.)
2. You justify his bad behavior with excuses like this:
   a) He's stressed out at work.
   b) His ex-wife wants alimony.
   c) His grown children have issues.

    d) He has depression and is off his meds.

    e) I'm too needy, demanding, bitchy. I must've driven him to this execrable behavior.

3. Eventually you can't take it anymore and explode.

4. The Asshat punishes you by icing you out for days at a time.

5. You apologize for blowing up.

6. Eventually, when he needs something from you, like favors, money, emotional support or sex, he returns.

7. You get back to care*taking*, he gets back to Asshattery and the cycle repeats.

The reality is … you're addicted to your man. If you were a food addict, he'd be your 600-calorie Chaco Taco.

He's as damaging to your mental health as any drug can be, because you simply can't resist mainlining him no matter how crappy his behavior.

<u>Change #6</u>: We're Unhappy All the Time.

We feel desperate, grasping and fated to live our lives forever disappointed or alone. And because of this …

> **"It's very tempting when you really want to be with someone to settle for much, much less - even a vague pathetic facsimile of less - than you would have ever imagined." -- *He's Just Not That Into You*, by Greg Behrendt & Liz Tuccillo**

I agree with Behrendt and Tuccillo. Your Asshat might not be that into you. But he's also an Asshat for not cutting you loose!

Recognizing the ways we've changed because of our relationship can be depressing and painful, but never fear. This information is essential in lighting a fire under our butts to get us working in The Solution.

SEVEN TACTICS I TRIED TO CHANGE MY MAN

Before I began working my recovery path I thought I could deal with my addiction to the Asshat and the cycle of abuse alone.

After all, I'd been senior class president and Homecoming Queen, graduating high school with high honors and eight college units because I slayed the Advanced Placement exams!

Plus, I'd spent my childhood helping my mom through her toxic marriage.

How hard could it be to cajole, finagle, hijack, manipulate, extort, bribe and browbeat my Asshat into loving me?

Apparently really stinking hard!

Tactic #1: I tried the "Love Letter Technique" from John Gray's _Men Are from Mars, Women Are from Venus_.

This technique was designed by Gray to help Venusians reconnect with their Martians after a fight.

While the Martian is in his lair, the Venusian is supposed to write a specific message that is supposed to get a positive response. Here's how I wrote mine:

I Expressed My Anger

"I'm angry because I snooped on your cell phone and found a photograph of you hugging your ex-girlfriend at your job last week.
"This makes me want to punch you in the throat."

I Expressed My Sadness

"I'm sad that you're still (possibly?) cheating on me when I'm trying so hard to make this relationship work by completely abandoning myself."

I Expressed My Fear

"I'm afraid that no matter how many *Love Letters* I write, you'll never change. I'll never marry or have children.
"I'll end up penniless, killed by a trolley car in Barcelona just like Antoni Gaudi, the unappreciated architect who beautified that ungrateful, Asshat city.
"I'm afraid that my love is simply pearls before swine. I'm also a little afraid of my own grandiosity."

I Expressed My Regret

"I regret being mad at you for continuously cheating on me. I don't want to make you run away.
"I'd rather heal you and make you whole. Because *that's* possible. Then we can live happily ever after."

I Expressed My Love

"I love you so much! Not for the man you are, but for the man I want you to be. Which I'm fabricating in my mind."

After all that rigmarole, Gray suggests we write ourselves a *Response* Letter.

Yes. We're supposed to write ourselves *exactly* the response we'd like to get from our knavish man in the cave. I wrote about a kajillion of those, too.

Because *that's* not completely insane!

Let's pause a moment here and picture a grown-ass 30-year old woman, alone in her house, writing Love Letters and Response Letters to her philandering boyfriend who has no idea *any* of this is going on because he's off arresting criminals and laying wenches.

Then, after said-woman has dotted every "I" and crossed every "T" in her myriad epistles, she finally gives them to her Asshat.

He says he'll read them later. She finds them in the trash unread, next to an empty bottle of his Aqua Velva.

Man, I've learned to love that poor, scrabbling, addicted girl.

Tactic #2: I Pretended to Be Very Busy!

I'm Just Mastering My Pyramid Bow Technique. Because That Isn't Totally Insane!

When Mister C.H. finally came out of his cave and called — hours, sometimes *days* after he said he would — I'd answer the phone and try to sound occupied and important. As if I had an actual *life* outside my obsession with him.

"Hello? Who is this? ... Oh, Mister C.H., the man who is supposed to be my boyfriend who I haven't heard from in five days."

(Crazy laughter verging on cackling.)

"Sorry, I was so busy macramé-ing table-runners that I didn't realize you still exist! Hey ... who's that ringing my doorbell?...

"Oh, look! It's my hot neighbor Harold-the-Surgeon." (It was actually my hot neighbor Barbara-the-Stenographer.)

I went so far as to take up hobbies I despised, like glue-gunning my own Christmas wreaths, just to seem busy.

I pretended to enjoy accidentally welding my fingers together with scorching Elmer's glue while, the whole time; I was dying a little inside.

If I were just more aloof, I thought, *Mister C.H. would snap back like a rubber band!*

(Don't even get me *started* on Gray's "rubber band" theory. Seriously, just don't.)

But somehow Mister C.H. could smell my insecurity the way a horse smells fear. You just can't wash that *Eau du Desperacion* off.

Tactic #3: I Tried Psychoanalyzing My Man ... for Free!

I helped Mister C.H. understand how his childhood difficulties had affected him.

I tried to make him see that our "True Love" could keep him from ending up exactly like the dysfunctional people in his family.

My Professional Opinion? He's a Fucking Mess!

He helped me understand that I couldn't blame him for his inconsistency, since *he* grew up with inconsistency. *Didn't I understand?*

Yes, I did. Somehow he used my very own manipulative wisdom against me!

Tactic #4: I Tried Auditioning for Wife.

After my man and I moved in together I turned our home into a cozy little love nest, aka Man Trap.

I bought Shabby Chic couches and Wild Oats groceries. I cooked Spaghetti Bolognese, hung wall art and rescued two dogs I hoped would serve as our practice children.

I did everything in my power to make Mister C.H. understand what an incredible wife and mother I'd make.

His response was to take as many overtime shifts as possible to escape my smothering domesticity.

Tactic #5: I Tried Being a 24-Hour Convenience Store for Sex.

During our five-year relationship, I denied Mister C.H. sex *once*, because I'd sprained my VaJayLaw from vigorous horseback trotting.

I was terrified to say "no" because he'd confessed that one of his greatest fears about marriage was that the sex would stop.

So, I made sure he knew that it was gonna be *all sex, all the time* with me.

Neither snow, nor rain, nor heat, nor gloom of night, nor the winds of gassy bloat, nor a menstrual-cycle-challenged body, would stay me from the swift completion of my appointed sexual favors.

I thought if I were the best lover my guy ever had, he'd realize marriage to me would be orgasmic bliss and *then* he'd change.

(By the way, my quest for bliss made for some pretty lame, anxious, forced sex.)

Tactic #6: I Tried to Convince Him That *I* Was Right.

When we're in a relationship with an Asshat we're perpetually disappointed. And because his behavior *is* disappointing we're also perpetually righteous.

I knew all the things Mister C.H. *should* and *shouldn't* be doing. There were lots of little things:

* He *shouldn't* take a bad day out on me.
* He *should* be less moody and mute.
* He *should* be consistent.
* He *should* be more affectionate.
* He *should* be less secretive. Was he secretive because there were "other women"?
* If so, he *should* give them up.

The whopper was this one:

* He *should* go to therapy to heal his childhood wounds so he could finally commit to and marry me!

I was right! *Anybody* could see I was right! Anybody but the Asshat, of course.

Tactic #7: I Tried Forcing Him to Come to Couples Counseling With Me.

Couples counseling *can* be incredibly helpful when both partners are invested in making the relationship work.

But dragging Mister C.H. to a counselor's office just prolonged a glaringly dysfunctional situation.

Mister C.H. knew exactly what our therapist wanted to hear, which was that he was damaged by his childhood, and with her help could perhaps fix it.

He said he *did* want to work up to marrying me ... someday. Our therapist was encouraged by his humility and willingness, but once we left the office, nothing ever changed.

I believe Mister C.H. agreed to participate in couples counseling because I met many of his emotional and physical needs and he wasn't ready to give that up.

I also suspect he wanted to *want* to get married, have kids and live what is considered a "traditional" lifestyle.

But all his behavior indicated that sexual fidelity and marriage to me scared him to death.

This is not to say that every man who *doesn't* want marriage and children is an Asshat. There's no rule that says any man (or woman) *has* to get married and have children to be emotionally healthy and have a fulfilling, happy life.

There are plenty of wonderful people who've done neither and are more evolved and enlightened than the best marrieds and parents around.

A Man Is an Asshat Only When He Lies About What He Wants to Use You to Fulfill His Emotional and Sexual Needs.

FIVE FEARS THAT KEEP US PARALYZED

We aren't staying in our toxic relationships because we're masochists.

True, we're putting up with some pretty egregious behavior and always coming back for more, but fear is a powerful motivator when it comes to having a death grip (literally) on our man.

Fear #1: The Devil We Know vs. the Devil We Don't Know

There comes a point in every toxic relationship where the cycle of abuse becomes habitual.

We simply get desensitized to the chicanery. And the thought of going back out on the Love Market is intimidating and demoralizing because we don't trust our Man Picker.

After all, we picked *this* guy. Who's to say the next one will be any better? In fact, we fear the next guy may be *worse*!

When you start thinking you've arrived at the last gas station in the desert it's pretty tough to risk taking off again.

This does not have to be true!

The more we work on our emotional health, the better our Man Picker will become.

In Twelve Step recovery, it's suggested we NOT make any drastic decisions for six months from the date we begin to work the program.

This includes leaving our current love interest and/or dating someone new.

We must be sure we're ready to leave our current situation and hone our self-love skills enough to reset our Man Picker.

Fear #2: We're Afraid if We Leave the Toxic Relationship We'll *Never* Have Kids.

Turning thirty was my Come-to-Jesus moment. I knew I wanted a family and my ovaries started yelling at me.

"What're you doing with this non-commital guy? You need to get serious, stat! Do you think we're going to be producing eggs forever?"

I made a forceful break-up speech to Mister C.H. And the guy just smiled.

He informed me that I was foolish to throw out our three-year relationship because it would take *at least* that long for me to meet another guy who may or may not want me.

And probably *double* that time to convince the new guy to marry and have kids with me. And by *that* time I probably wouldn't even be *able* to have kids.

Talk about emotional blackmail.

Given the glacial pace of our relationship, I decided Mister C.H. was probably right so I stayed — *two more years!*

One Last Thought About Kids

Working the 12 life-altering exercises you'll find in The Solution made me ask myself the hard questions about bringing a child into a calamitous environment.

I tried to imagine how that child would be affected by living in a home with parents doing the Dance-of-Death?

> **_Dance-of-Death_: - A Symbolic Dance in Which Death, Represented as a Skeleton, Leads People to Their Graves."**
> **– Webster's Dictionary**

I worried my unborn child might feel like he or she had to take care of me, the way I'd taken care of my mom during her emotionally abusive relationship.

I realized that if I married Mister C.H. I'd be duplicating my mom's second marriage and that my child would likely inherit some of my dysfunctional traits; like low self-esteem, codependency disorder and love addiction.

So, when your fear of ending up childless kicks in, take a deep breath and remember, it's not enough to give birth to a child.

You want more than that. Ideally you'd like a loving, supportive, stable home to raise that child in.

Don't put the cart before the horse. Don't let your biology pressure you into repeating generational dysfunction.

Heal yourself first then leave the door open for a child to enter your life by any wonderful means possible.

Caveat: For those of you who _already_ have children with an Asshat, fear not.

When you walk through the exercises in The Solution you'll show your kids, by example, what self-love looks like.

Be transparent with your process, as is appropriate for their age, and do *not* allow your disease of codependency to cause you to lie to or neglect your children.

Most of all be kind to yourself. You're doing the best you can, one day at a time. We're looking for:

Progress, Not Perfection! – Twelve Step Slogan

Fear #3: We're Afraid That It's a Bad Time to Hold Our Asshat Accountable for His Asshattery.

Those of us afflicted with care*taking* tendencies, pride ourselves on our ability to make other people feel good. So, it's tough to confront them once and for all about their destructive behavior.

A Toxic Friendship

Let's give men a rest for the moment. I had a friendship with a *woman* that was more difficult than any of my love affairs. Let's call her Amanda.

I met Amanda in the college dorms my freshman year. I could tell right away she was an emotional vampire and tried to flee her clutches.

But Amanda could smell my people-pleasing, doormat-ishness from five doors down. She basically forced me to be her friend (aka slave) by coming into my room, grabbing me by the arm and making me go places with her.

She also seemed to need a lot of favors. Which turned out to be very exhausting for me. "No" was not a word in my vocabulary at the time.

Here are the things I did for Amanda:

* Held her head while she vomited in 20 different nightclubs over 10 years.
* Drove her to one of her four abortions then cooked and cleaned while she recuperated.
* Helped her move apartments five times. (I still bear a scar on the top of my foot caused by her 500-pound armoire.)

My Low Point?

Hiding behind my sofa while she banged on my front door and peered through my window trying to find me.

There's more, but I'll stop.

Ironically, it was my friendship with Amanda, not my dysfunctional love affairs that finally drove me into therapy.

In my very first session, my therapist told me flat out that I had to get out of the friendship.

"I want to," I replied. "But this is a really bad time for Amanda. Her boyfriend just kicked her out and she wants to stay on my couch until she can get herself together."

To which my therapist asked, "Is there *ever* a good time for Amanda?"

Hmm. Actually. No.

I didn't have the cajones to end the friendship in person. I hand-wrote a five-page letter detailing my reasons for bidding her adieu, then spent a year hiding behind my couch every time someone knocked on the front door.

I saw you hiding behind your ⟶ couch!!

I want to sell ← you to gypsies!

The bottom line: It's *never* a good time to confront or detach from a toxic person. Especially an Asshat.

Sometimes, as the mentally questionable Shia LeBeouf attested to in his motivational video, you've got to *"Just do it!"*

So, when you're afraid it's a bad time to hold an Asshat accountable and are drowning in a sea of your own misplaced empathy, remember he has his own spiritual journey.

To alleviate your codependent guilt, apply this excellent motto to your guy.

"It's Not (His) Fault That (He's) Fucked Up; But It <u>Is</u> (His) Fault if (He) Stays Fucked Up." -- Jen Sincero, author of *You Are A Badass*

Fear #4: We're Afraid the Asshat Will Die Without Us

This is Fear #3 on crack.

We're especially susceptible to this fear if we once felt responsible for a parent who was addicted to drugs, alcohol or abusive relationships when we were growing up.

As I struggled to extricate myself from Mister C.H., I felt deep dread that without me he'd become a devastated husk of a man.

After all, hadn't he begged me to take him back with tears in his eyes? *Would he be okay without me?*

I remember sitting in church after our break-up, weeping my eyes out as I prayed to God to take care of my fragile ex-boyfriend who'd done everything he could to destroy our relationship and me.

After two weeks of sheer, guilty hell, I came home from work to discover a note tucked into my screen door from Mister C.H.'s *new girlfriend,* Jeri, who was already doing the Dance-of-Death with him and was desperate for advice.

I don't want to be dismissive. I'm sure there are instances where a jilted toxic person does *indeed* self-harm. But let's remember:

The 3 Cs of Acceptance: You didn't <u>Cause</u> your toxic partner's dysfunction. You can't <u>Control</u> it. And you can't <u>Cure</u> it.

Have you tattooed that on your butt yet? Get to it!

<u>Fear #5</u>: We're Afraid Our Man Will Take Everything He Learned From Us and Give It to the Next Girl.

Did Mister C.H. suddenly do an about-face for his next girlfriend, Jeri?

Not according to that note she left in my screen door. She asked if I knew whether Mister C.H. had "secret girlfriends" and implored me to call her back.

When I talked to her on the phone I had just one word of advice:

"Run!"

It's not our business to think about whether our guy will change when we leave him. Our only business is to continue *our* own journey to emotional health, making positive changes in ourselves.

I've given examples of five fears that keep us stuck in toxic relationships.

But, there are many more unique to each of us, and it's *our* responsibility to ferret them out, check their validity and ask ourselves how we'll manage if they happen to be true.

This next chapter is going to prepare us to step into The Solution and kick some recovery butt.

SIX ESSENTIAL ATTITUDES FOR RECOVERY

When it comes to recovery attitude is everything.

It's the difference between defending, justifying and blaming others for our codependent behaviors, and seeing recovery as a positive opportunity to change ourselves to invite and nurture Real Love.

With this in mind, what follows are six *essential* attitudes to adopt when you begin recovery.

Attitude #1: Humility

It's only when we get *truly* humble that we're willing to dig deep and take an unvarnished look at ourselves.

Humility helps us to "get real" and get rid of the pride and denial that's keeping us stuck.

It might feel counter-intuitive to "get humble" while in your emotionally toxic relationship. After all, how much more humble are you supposed to become?

You're already putting up with emotional abuse. Doesn't that mean you're already pretty humble? The answer is "no." Humiliation and Humility are entirely different concepts.

Humiliation is shaming

It occurs when we do something self-destructive, or allow another person to destroy us emotionally, spiritually and/or physically.

Humility is powerlessness

It occurs when we admit that we have absolutely *no idea* what the hell we're doing when it comes to our love lives, and become willing to ask for help.

It takes a great deal of stubbornness to hang onto the wild bucking bronco of a toxic relationship.

We *say* we want a healthy relationship and Real Love with a good man, but we choose to try to break and shape the one we've got into the person we want him to be.

And we're too proud to leave our relationship because we want to prove all the naysayers wrong.

If we were humble and accepted that there was no *way* we could fundamentally change our guy and that we had *no control* over our addiction to him and the cycle of abuse, *then* we'd be willing to ask for help.

Humility reminds us we're not responsible for, nor capable of changing or controlling other people's behavior.

So, as we work through the exercises in The Solution, I'm going to ask you to let go of your pride and admit defeat.

It will be a relief to know, for once and for all, that you don't have to keep paddling that relationship kayak upstream.

When you stop rowing your man will either pick up the oars and start doing his share of the work or you'll just float away from him, without resistance, and see where you come ashore.

Pride Is the Façade We Use to Hide Our Fear, Sorrow, Emptiness, Insecurity and Self-Loathing.

Attitude #2: Willingness

We must become willing in our recovery to take responsibility for our own lives and stop blaming other people

Oh, how I blamed my Asshats! They were torturing me, after all. Why didn't they just get their shit together so I could be happy??

And, let's see, who else did I blame? I know — my parents!

"Mom, Dad, Hi, it's me.

"Yes, I know it's four in the morning, but Mister C.H. *still* hasn't come home yet. I've texted and called and he's not answering and maybe he's off with some other woman.

"Oh, *why* does this always happen to me? Maybe if you guys hadn't divorced and damaged me I'd be okay.

"Yes, I know I'm 30-years-old and it's my life now, but you guys really messed me up and you should pay until you die. If only I'd had a happier childhood!"

It's true many of my codependent behaviors were picked up in childhood. But this is where I had to apply the Jen Sincero quote to

myself. It wasn't my fault I was fucked up, but it *was* certainly my fault if I chose to remain fucked up.

No matter how difficult our childhood, we must become willing to look at it. Grieve it. Confront perpetrators once, if need be.

Weep. Moan. Gnash our teeth. Get counseling. Cry. Roll on the ground. Stomp our feet. Own it. Then let it go.

It could take six months. It could take six years. But ...

Our Ultimate Goal Is to Stop Blaming Anyone Else for the State of Our Current Life.

Like a hit of gin, blame feels good in the moment, but leaves us with a spiritual hangover. It also ends up making us loathe ourselves.

So now that you're adopting humility and are willing to take responsibility for your own life, we move on to ...

Attitude #3: Shamelessness

Shame exists for a reason. It stops us from doing reprehensible things.

However, for those of us engaged in emotionally abusive relationships, shame can keep us silent and hiding. We've got to be shame*less* by admitting what's really going on in our lives to people who can help us.

"You're Only as Sick as Your Secrets" -- Twelve-Step slogan

This kind of transparency can be daunting.

If you take a peek at pretty much any social media site, nine times out of 10 you're going to see the *curated lives* of people who *seem to* be emotionally healthy, happy and enviable.

Those people get my panties in a bunch because I'm comparing the inside of my messy life to the outside of their seemingly perfect lives.

Nobody wants to tell the truth about how challenged they really are!

But if you want to get healthy, intrepid Recovery Road-Warrior, you're gonna have to fess up, in a *safe place* with people who can help you recover.

No more secrets. To become transparent, you've got to deal with your shame.

The clients I work with come from all walks of life. Some are blue collar, some were born feasting off silver spoons; some are ingénues (20s), others, leading ladies (60s). Some are dating; others are married.

And shame is the thread that connects them all.

* They're ashamed that they're in or attract toxic relationships.
* They're ashamed they can't go "cold turkey" and get out for good.
* They believe they're stupid, worthless and unlovable.
* They are Human Doings rather than Human Beings. For example: *I will tap dance to make you love me. I will fix you to make you love me. I'll be loyal no matter how badly you treat me to make you love me.*

Mary's Story

Mary was four when her alcoholic mother divorced her father. She then became her mom's caretaker.

This included putting mom to bed after she passed out, calling in sick for her when she was hung over and feeding and dressing her; a tall order for a child. This taught Mary that her only value was in helping her mother stay sober and safe.

When Mary was 12 her mom went to rehab and Mary moved in with her dad and his second family.

Mary's "child mind" interpreted her mom's departure as proof of Mary's fundamental worthlessness.

In her dad's home, Mary was told she had "no common sense," that she was "too sensitive" and that she was "smart in school, but dumb in life."

Mary learned there was an "absolute right way" to do things and that much of the time she got it wrong and needed to be taught how to do it correctly over and over.

This made Mary feel ashamed for just being herself.

When Mary came to me, the first thing we had to work on was her shame. She needed to get out of denial, accept her broken parts and feel worthy of embracing recovery.

I tell clients it's impossible to get rid of shame completely — and we can even be ashamed that we can't get rid of shame — but we *can* learn to manage it.

I suggest my clients make "shame" a person and try to find an image that fits.

Here's what mine looks like:

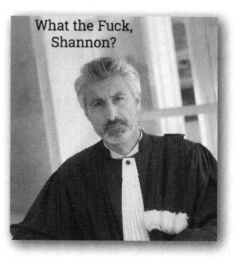

What the Fuck, Shannon?

Like mine, Mary's shame is a man. He wears a business suit and tie.

He knows everything Mary doesn't know.

He especially knows that Mary is incapable, stupid and unworthy of love.

So when Shame walks in the door, wearing his Bruno Magli shoes and his judgmental, scowling face, Mary says this:

"Hello Shame, I see you're here to make me feel bad and keep me from enjoying my life. I know you won't leave and that's fine, because I'm going to do what I set out to do, even if you tag along.

"And for the record, I'm worthy of love today. I'm responsible today. I'm conscientious today. I will not let you, or my past, define me."

Personifying shame helps us see the small, worthless nothing inside the big, scary monster, like the Great and Powerful Wizard of Oz.

We Have Our Shame, but We Are <u>Not</u> Our Shame.

And it's very powerful when we share our shame with other people. Dr. Robert Caldwell of *Psych Sight* notes:

"There is nothing shameful about shame. You have every right to yours. You earned it by surviving in the midst of shaming people.

"There is a great community of the shamed waiting to dare to trust others enough to be open and vulnerable.

"Sharing your shame with them will be a way of forming strong and rejuvenating ties with others."

Sharing our shame also lightens our psychic load and allows self-compassion to enter. In this instance, becoming shameless is a good thing.

<u>Attitude #4</u>: Self-Compassion

Peeling the Denial Onion can be approached in two different ways:

* Through self-criticism or
* Through self-compassion

Self-criticism can lead to relapse in our addiction and inflame our low self-esteem.

In her *Psychology Today* article, Dr. Leslie Becker-Phelps says this:

"Those who are self-compassionate gain more benefits from introspection than their self-critical counterparts.

"Although the search-and-destroy missions of self-critical people are certainly a direct way to move through personal difficulties and advance toward goals, they can be extremely stressful and tiring.

"To make things worse, self-critical individuals are essentially attacking themselves; they are their own victims."

By contrast, Becker-Phelps writes, people who are highly self-compassionate comfort themselves at the same time they recognize their challenges and failures, which leads to acceptance and change.

Self-compassionate people can see themselves more clearly. Self-critical people tend to be more defensive, which keeps them stuck.

Here's an example of what the critical inner voice might say:

"You are *such* a loser when it comes to relationships, Shannon. You've got to snap out of it, right now!"

While the self-compassionate voice would say:

"Shannon, I'm so proud of how hard you're working to heal the wounds that invite difficult relationships into your life. Be very patient with yourself throughout this process, because you are valuable and lovable exactly as you are right now."

Doesn't the compassionate voice make you feel less ashamed and overwhelmed and more inspired and hopeful?

And for the record, the self-compassionate voice is telling the truth. Scout's honor.

Attitude #5: Bravery

In the beginning, recovery hurts because all the toxic stuff you've repressed to survive will rise to the surface.

This is when we must gird our loins and become brave enough to feel our Origin Feelings instead of masking them.

When we're addicted to the cycle of abuse, chances are we've been numbing out our feelings of worthlessness and shame.

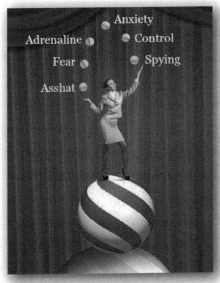

We've most likely been keeping ourselves preoccupied with masking feelings like Control, Fear, Obsession and more. It looks a little bit like this:

As long as we're juggling these Masking Feelings and engaging in compulsive behavior, we can't excavate our Origin Feelings.

And let's face it, being an obsessive control freak ain't fun, but we think it beats dealing with the alternative:

* Our Rage
* And beneath our Rage, our Sadness
* And beneath our Sadness, our Shame
* And beneath our Shame, our Grief

And for some of us anger, sadness, shame and grief, can be terrifying.

We can be afraid that if we let those feelings out they just might obliterate us off the face of the earth.

That's why starting recovery is such a *brave* thing to do, because it asks us to *feel* our Origin Feelings.

If these feelings are too big, especially if you've suffered physical or sexual abuse as a child, you'll need a mental health professional to help you navigate them in a safe way.

You also don't have to let your origin feelings out all at once.

Pace yourself. Let them come forward just a little bit at a time, day after day, week after week until they've had their day in the sun and can finally begin to dissipate.

Because those feelings will guide us to address the real problem, which is that somewhere in our childhood we were damaged.

* Some of us learned we weren't good enough.
* Some of us learned we were shameful.
* Some of us learned that our bodies weren't our own.
* Some of us learned we couldn't trust the people we loved.
* Some of us learned that all we could expect from life was abuse.
* Some of us learned to have *no* needs, and to fill the needs of others.
* Some of us learned we could survive if we *didn't* show our emotions or, better yet, didn't *have* any emotions.

In Childhood We Were Too Young to Understand That It Wasn't Our Fault.

As adults, many of us *intellectually* understand our childhood damage isn't our fault. But that angry, scared, shamed, sad inner child (more on her in The Solution) still believes it is.

This is where the real work begins. We must solve the real problem by grieving our childhood. And grieving *hurts*.

Why Grieving Is So Important!

Psychologist Donald L. Anderson, author of *Better than Blessed*, writes:

> "Healthy are those who mourn. Only very recently have we begun to realize that to deny grief is to deny a natural human function and that such denial sometimes produces dire consequences.
>
> "Grief, like any genuine emotion, is accompanied by certain physical changes and the release of a form of psychic energy.
>
> "If that energy is not expended in the normal process of grieving, it becomes destructive within the person. Even physical illness can be a penalty for unresolved grief."

I believe we can also suffer a soul sickness if we don't release our grief. But as painful as grief is, it is one of the essential tools for moving us to recovery.

Attitude #6: Gratitude

When we're in the pits of Asshat Hell, it's very difficult to feel any gratitude.

In fact, we are likely filled with jealousy and scorn toward those we *imagine* have great relationships. The inside of our head may sound something like this:

> "My sister is five years younger than me and she's already married with three kids to a great guy who treats her like a queen. What's so wonderful about her? How come she's not messed up like me? Especially since we grew up in the same house!"

Or …

"My best friend is going to Europe. Her husband is taking her. Meanwhile my guy won't even take me on an overnighter to Muskogee, Oklahoma! What's so great about her anyway? She's flat-chested and has large teeth!"

And those are some of the more *charitable* thoughts we might have when we're jealous of someone who seemingly has all that we desire.

When we're in this state of mind we're miserable. We dislike ourselves even more than we dislike the people we're jealous of, which makes it incredibly difficult to get better.

We're Ingesting the Emotional Poison of "Compare and Despair."

This is where the powerful practice of Gratitude comes in. In her book, *The Magic*, author Rhonda Byrne presents this Bible verse:

"Whoever has gratitude will be given more, and he or she will have an abundance. Whoever does not have gratitude, even what he or she has will be taken from him or her."

Byrne's interpretation:

"If you don't take the time to be grateful you will never have more, and what you do have you will lose."

For those of us who'd rather not dally about with religious texts, Byrne also cites Sir Isaac Newton's *Law of Attraction*.

"The 'Law of Attraction' ... governs all the energy in our Universe, from the formation of an atom to the movement of the planets, 'like attracts like.'

"In your life, the law operates on your thoughts and feelings, because they are energy, too. So, whatever you think, whatever you feel, you attract."

I want to be clear that I'm not suggesting you be grateful for your toxic relationship or the emotional abuse happening in it.

I'm asking you to be rigorously grateful for what's *good* in your life. Here's how you start:

Task: Write down 10 things you're grateful for every night before you go to bed or every morning before you get up.

The gratitude list I wrote from the depths of dysfunctional despair:

1. I'm grateful for the loving girlfriends in my life who always have my back.
2. I'm grateful to be financially self-supporting.
3. I'm grateful for my dogs Wyatt and Shelby and their wet noses and sweet doggy butt-breath kisses.
4. I'm grateful that my car works.
5. I'm grateful to live in America where I have the luxury of pursuing emotional health.
6. I'm grateful that I live only a mile from the beach and it's free!
7. I'm grateful for the scent of night-blooming jasmine.
8. I'm grateful for Brad Pitt and how easy on the eyes he is.
9. I'm grateful for dance parties.
10. I'm grateful for my willingness to try to get better and my fortitude in going for it, despite doubt and fear.

And my list went on. Sometimes, after I'd done my list for the day, I read it aloud. And when I did this I actually *did* begin to feel grateful, even though I remained a bit jaded about the task.

One example of faux gratitude launched at my Asshat:

> **"I love you so much! Not for the person you <u>actually</u> are, but for the person I want you to be. Which I am fabricating in my mind."**

If you're as cynical as I was, there's another great Twelve Step slogan you can tattoo on your forearm:

Fake It 'Til You Make It!

Now, with our wonderful attitudes in place it's officially time to move on to The Solution portion of this program!

Yeehaw and Yippee Ki-Yay!!

PART TWO:

❖ ❖ ❖

THE SOLUTION

TOOLS YOU'LL NEED FOR *THE SOLUTION*

Tool #1: The Twelve Steps of Recovery

In 1935 Bill Wilson and Bob Smith founded Alcoholics Anonymous (AA) in Akron, Ohio with the idea that *mutual support in a spiritual program* could heal addiction and they created the Twelve Steps as their True North.

Since then, Twelve Step recovery has blossomed into as many as thirty-five other programs to manage almost any addiction you can name and is considered among the best approaches to both physical and emotional sobriety.

The Twelve Steps are where I started my recovery so they inform many of the exercises I offer in The Solution.

I've been given permission to reprint the steps for my uses by the mother program, AA.

I prefer to use the words "Higher Power" in place of the word "God," as the latter word can be freighted for many people. And I've replaced the word "alcohol" with "Asshats" to keep it specific to us.

Beneath each step I'm going to give you my interpretation of what we're meant to do.

Different people will have different interpretations and ways of working the steps. I'm offering you what worked for me:

The Twelve Steps

Step One: **We admitted we were powerless over others [Asshats] - that our lives had become unmanageable.**

We take this step when we've hit rock bottom and recognize we have no idea how to fix our relationship issues.

Embracing this step means we're ready to do things differently than we ever have before. We're ready to take radical action.

Step Two: **Came to believe that a power greater than ourselves could restore us to sanity.**

If we've been religious before, but feel the God of our religion isn't helping, we're ready to look for a *new definition* of God.

Even if we're agnostic or atheistic, we've come to the conclusion that we can't fix our brain with our brain. We're willing to suspend our cynicism and disbelief to find a Higher Power of "our own" understanding.

Step Three: **Made a decision to turn our will and lives over to the care of our Higher Power as we understood him.**

We take this step when we recognize that nothing we've tried to control our Asshat and our addiction to the emotional cycle of abuse has worked.

We're ready to give up control and let someone else take the wheel. (And it doesn't have to be Jesus, unless that works for you.)

Step Four: Made a searching and fearless moral inventory of ourselves.

We take this step when we recognize that we are the common denominator in all our codependent relationships and that the only person we can change is ourselves.

So we roll up our sleeves to do the arduous work of discovering what character traits keep us in Asshat Hell.

Step Five: Admitted to our Higher Power, to ourselves, and to another human being, the exact nature of our wrongs.

We take this step when we are ready to move out of shame and isolation so we can recover.

Step Six: Were entirely ready to have our Higher Power remove all these defects of character.

Usually we hang on to our "defects of character" (i.e., care*taking*, controlling, manipulating) because we're afraid of what will happen if we let them go.

We take this step when we want to be able to walk through our fears to a new freedom.

Step Seven: Humbly asked our Higher Power to remove our shortcomings.

We take this step when we are finally ready to let go of our self-defeating traits and leave the results to our Higher Power.

Step Eight: Made a list of all persons we had harmed and became willing to make amends to them all.

We take this step when we are no longer dogged by shame and are ready to apologize to people who have been hurt by our addiction to Asshats and the emotional cycle of abuse.

These may include our parents, our siblings, our children and our friends. But, more often than not, we must make amends to ourselves and our inner child. (More on her later.)

Step Nine: Made direct amends to such people wherever possible, except when to do so would injure them or others.

We take this step when we feel certain we will no longer engage in the destructive behavior.

Step Ten: Continued to take personal inventory and when we were wrong, promptly admitted it.

Step Eleven: Sought through prayer and meditation to improve our conscious contact with our Higher Power as we understood him, praying only for knowledge of our Higher Power's will for us and the power to carry that out.

We are ready for Steps Ten and Eleven when we've worked all the previous steps and have decided to adopt them as an ongoing spiritual practice and lifestyle change.

Step Twelve: Having had a spiritual awakening as the result of these steps, we tried to carry this message to other sufferers, and to practice these principles in all our affairs.

We take this step when other people ask us how we've come to be so functional and awesome. We don't need to proselytize.

In every Twelve Step program "attraction, rather than promotion" is the cornerstone of helping others, and practitioners have learned that when they volunteer to help others they're less likely to relapse.

What's great about these steps is that you can do them in order or you can skip around, depending on which seem pertinent at that moment in your life.

You can also work the steps more than once. You'll find that each time you work through the steps, another layer of the Denial Onion will be peeled back to facilitate greater self-awareness and healing.

FYI, there's no perfect way to work the steps. Remember, it's about progress, not perfection.

Tool #2: Your Asshat Recovery Notebook

It's time to purchase something you can write in.

It can be all fancy and expensive and girly with your name embossed in gold leaf on the cover and peppy slogans in Sanskrit font on each page, or it can be a simple lined yellow legal pad.

Either way this will be your Asshat Recovery Notebook wherein you'll journal like a fiend.

Journaling *by hand* is preferred. Because, in my experience, the practice gives us access to our unconscious brain, which harbors thoughts and feelings we were unaware of.

(If you can only do your journaling at work on your computer, so be it. This is not an All-Or-Nothing-At-All situation.)

As you journal, obsolete ideas, old, unhelpful belief systems and longstanding issues will appear, as if by sleight of hand, onto the page.

You might even think, *Who the hell wrote that? Could that be me?* It can. It is. And it's okay.

Keep your Asshat Recovery Notebook hidden, but handy. You'll need to refer to it as you work the subsequent exercises.

You might feel resistance to some of these exercises and tasks. If so, skip over the ones you don't relate to or don't want to do and work the ones you like.

You may decide to come back to the ones you skipped later. There's no perfect way to do these tasks. Just remember to:

"Take What You Like and Leave the Rest" – Twelve-Step Slogan

Each time you walk through these exercises, you'll peel more and more of the Denial Onion, which allows greater insights and recovery to flood in.

Which brings me to the first, powerful exercise in The Solution.

EXERCISE ONE: CREATE YOUR PERFECT MATE

There's been a great deal of research that says goal-setting has transformative powers. In his *Psychology Today* article, "7 Steps to Get What You Want," Dr. Brad Klontz writes:

"Without a clear vision of what we want to achieve, we will be unable to reach our full potential.

"Without a vision of what we want, we have little hope of creating an ideal relationship, finding a dream job or acquiring whatever else we think will bring us joy.

"Most important, without goals, we are unable to unleash our vast store of subconscious resources that have the power to help us create our ideal world."

Which leads us to …

Task A: Write down the "Top 10 Qualities" you want in a romantic partner. No matter how eccentric, oddball, weird and wonderful!

My Story

When my last therapist suggested I make my "Ideal Mate" list, I remember thinking it smacked of "magical thinking."

But when you're in emotional turmoil you'll try just about anything to feel better.

After I wrote my list I looked over at Mister C.H. - who lay sleeping in our bed as I furtively scribbled my S.O.S to the future - and realized he was *nowhere* to be found on my list.

This caught me by surprise. I thought certainly he'd have *some* of the qualities I desired in a romantic partner or what the heck was I doing with him?

I sank into a funk. By that time, I'd accepted that I was absolutely incapable of changing my guy into the person I described.

In a pitiful state, I put the list away and forgot about it … *for three whole years!!*

I unearthed it when I was packing my things to move in with Michael, my now-husband.

I sat down, reread it and realized with complete stupefaction that Michael fulfilled *every single one* of my requirements.

Writing the list worked on my unconscious brain and helped me become ready to invite a loving man into my life.

I must emphasize that my husband *isn't* perfect (neither am I), but he's perfect *for me*.

So, let the record show that the following described my ideal mate. Feel free to steal anything you like:

1. A faithful partner, which means no hookers and blow.
2. A partner who wants marriage and kids (before I'm 90).
3. A partner I can count on.
4. A partner who respects me, in the morning and always.
5. A partner who makes me laugh and thinks I'm as funny as *I* think I am!
6. A partner who makes me feel like I could do anything, even push-ups.
7. A partner who thinks I'm beautiful inside and out.
8. A partner who attracts me, not just physically, but morally and intellectually.
9. A partner who likes spending time with my friends and family and loves them.
10. A partner who is a good communicator, even from his cave.

Now it's time for you to Create Your Perfect Mate. Once you're done with that we'll move on to:

Task B: Prioritize your list.

Place the most important quality you're seeking in a partner at the top of the list and work your way down to the least important. Then:

Task C: Write down the values you discovered in your list

Our values are often forgotten during the *Sturm und Drang* of painful love affairs. We're just doing our best to keep our heads above water.

When I look at my own prioritized list I can see my values jumping up and down, doing The Whip and The Nae Nae to get my attention. They were:

Loyalty, Family, Respect, Humor, Wisdom, Community.

Look at your completed list. Do you see your values there waiting for you to embrace them?

Living in Our Values Is the Ultimate Goal to Set!

Once you've done tasks A-C, it's time to take our goal-setting one step further. We must set Highly Specific Goals.

Dr. Edwin Locke, American psychologist and pioneer in goal-setting theory has this to say about it:

"Setting specific goals (e.g., I want to earn $500 more a month) generates higher levels of performance than setting general goals e.g., I want to earn more money" … the harder the goal, the more a person will work to reach it."

They Forced Me to Set a Specific Goal!

I was so disconsolate with Mister C.H. that I paid a ton of money to go to a creepy self-help conference called *The Forum.*

It was held in a huge warehouse with flickering fluorescent lights and ominous booming noises emanating from the floor below.

(They said it was a video arcade??)

Bright-eyed minions brandishing clipboards herded attendees forward like cows into the slaughter chute! Fortunately, I survived.

The conference wasn't particularly life-altering, for better or worse, but one positive thing did come from that weekend.

I was asked to write down exactly what I wanted for my future. This is when I finally had to *admit* to myself and to others that I wanted to be married.

And as if *that* weren't painful enough, they *forced me* put a **Time Frame** on it!

That freaked me out. It made me feel like I had to leave Mister C.H. instantly, and I knew I wasn't ready for that.

But, I trembled at defying the Forum stooges.

I didn't want to end up in lockdown where David Miscavige, on hiatus from *Scientology*, would lash me with a thousand al dente spaghetti noodles. So, I wrote down the truth:

"I'd like to be married in five years."

Holy shit! *That* was scary!

For someone who kept saying she wanted a commitment, I was terrified of making one *to myself!*

It was in December 1995 that I set that goal. And I was smart enough to leave Mister. C.H. out of it.

I walked down the aisle in the most gorgeous organza wedding dress, my father weeping in relief as he escorted me, on May 27, 2001, a mere five months beyond my time frame!

Now it's your turn.

Task D: Write down in ink (!) the time frame in which you'd like to attract your perfect mate and what your life with him would look like!

For this task use visualization.

When I ask you what your life with your perfect mate looks like, I'm asking you to actually *see* that life.

Are there children? Is there a beautiful white house with a wrap-around veranda in the Seychelles? Is there a dog named Maximillian and a cat named Wally?

Visualization Is an Incredibly Powerful Tool for Attracting and Receiving What You Want in Life.

You can even make a vision collage, if you like. I chose photos that represented love, marriage, home and children.

Have a look:

Boy, did my critical voices have a heyday when I finished. "You want to get married and have kids? *How original!*"

Cynicism and shame just loooove to break up a good visualization. You may not be able to get those jerkwad critics to leave, but you can blow them off like you do your disgruntled Aunt Edith (or similar relative) who hates to see *anybody* happy.

Recap of Exercise One: Create Your Perfect Mate

Task A: Write down the Top 10 Qualities you want in a romantic partner. Be as specific as possible.

Task B: Prioritize your list based on the qualities you value most.

Task C: Write down your values.

Task D: Write down in ink (!) the time frame in which you'd like to attract your perfect mate and use visualization to picture how your life with him would look.

Onward, you brave, willing, transparent, intrepid one!

Quality & Priority #	Values Reflected
1. I want a man who is faithful to me.	Loyalty, Integrity
2.	
3.	
4.	
5.	
6.	
7.	
8.	

9.	
10.	

EXERCISE TWO: DOES HE ADD UP?

Now that you have your "Perfect Mate" written down, it's time to assess the qualities of your current partner.

<u>Task A</u>: Make a list of your partner's Pros and Cons.

Take your time. Don't rush. Write down all the reasons for staying with your current lad or not, accepting the fact that you *cannot* change him.

Here were a couple of my Pros:

* He's tall.
* He's a good lover.
* He's tidy.
* He smells good.
* He has a great job.

Here were some of my Cons:

* I don't trust him.
* He won't make plans.
* He sometimes ices me out for days and I don't know why.

* He flirts with other women in my presence.
* He takes and takes, but doesn't give.

Put your lists aside for a week or two so you can then review them objectively. Once enough time has passed, take a look.

Task B: Rank each Pro from 1-10, according to its value to you.

For instance, I scored 5 for "good lover." And 2 for "he's tidy."

Task C: Rank each Con from 1 and 10 based on what bothers you the most.

"I don't trust him and worry he's unfaithful" scored a 10. "He won't make plans with my friends and family" scored an 8.

Task D: Add the numbers up.

Compare your Cons number with your Pros number to see which side outweighs the other. Then ask yourself if you're willing to live the rest of your life with your guy *exactly as he is.*

When I did this task, my numbers were truly eye-opening:

* **Pros 19**
* **Cons 46**

Yikes! Now add on this last question: *Are you willing to bring children into the world that will have to live with him exactly as he is right now?*

Because guess what? Becoming a father also *does not* change the Asshat.

If he's inconsistent, unpredictable, unfaithful, angry and mean to you, he will, in all probability, be the same way with his children.

Perhaps even more daunting, your children could learn to behave exactly like him!

She Did It for Her "Children"

My client Cassandra had one of Oprah's patented "Aha!" moments sitting at a red light.

She was 32-years-old. It was 6 a.m. on a Saturday and she was on her way to a recovery meeting because her boyfriend wasn't speaking to her and she didn't know how long his stonewalling would last.

She distinctly remembered thinking how pitiful it was for an unmarried woman in her 30s to be heading to this meeting with a bunch of "losers" at such an un-Godly hour and on the weekend, no less.

Shouldn't she be tucked cozily in bed with a husband who loved her and their tow-headed children?

Or, at the very least, sleeping off a hangover from partying with fun, hot, jet-setting people instead of obsessing about her lover and whose bed he might be in at that very moment?

In fact, Cassie found the whole thing *so* demoralizing that she decided to whip a U-turn, go home, get back into bed and pull the covers over her head.

At that exact moment, the light turned green. But Cassie couldn't drive forward because a homeless woman had just pushed her grocery cart into the crosswalk.

Initially Cassie was impatient. She had a pity party to get back to.

Then she noticed that this disheveled woman was having an explosive argument with the voices in her head, gesticulating, stomping, cursing and pausing from time to time to shake an angry finger at her invisible foes.

Suddenly tears filled Cassie's eyes. She didn't instantly understand her emotions. Was she crying for this sad, lost stranger?

No.

Was she crying for herself, wondering if she might become just as crazy as that homeless woman if her current toxic relationship continued?

No.

Cassie realized she was crying *for her children*, the ones *who weren't even born yet*. Because Cassie realized if she married her current heartbreaker, their children might witness screaming arguments, thrown plates and sobbing jags.

She'd likely be preoccupied and angry most of the time. And eventually divorced and, if she wasn't careful, her children might end up as damaged and alone as that homeless lady.

That was Cassie's turning point. Maybe she didn't love herself enough to end her relationship, but she did love her *future children* enough to try everything within her power, including a 6 a.m. Twelve Step meeting to turn her life around.

Recap of Exercise Two: Does He Add Up?

Task A: Make a list of the Pros and Cons in your partner.

Task B: Rank each Pro between 1 and 10 according to what you value.

Task C: Rank each Con between 1 and 10, according to what most bothers you.

Task D: Add up the Pros and Cons to see how your man measures up.

Clarity Trumps Denial!

Note: This list-making is a process. Feel free to do this exercise multiple times.

EXERCISE THREE: BUILD YOUR MENTAL HEALTH VILLAGE

Addiction and toxic relationships are painful, embarrassing and can force us into hiding.

When you're in a damaging relationship you often isolate. And isolation is dangerous to our emotional health.

A huge component of *any* kind of recovery requires that we break out of our self-imposed prison and reach out to other people.

When it comes to kicking an Asshat addiction, you *must* move out of isolation by using:

The "3 Cs of Recovery" -- Community, Connection and Communication.

Just as it takes a village to raise a child, it also takes a village to raise our mental health. That one deserves its own marquee:

Raising Our Mental Health Takes a Village!

The next series of tasks aim to help you build your Mental Health Village.

Task A: Find a Trusted Advisor

A Trusted Advisor is a priceless touchstone who can witness and facilitate our healing.

Your Trusted Advisor should *not* be:

Your mom, dad, sister, children, gynecologist, bookie or *anyone* who has *an emotional investment* in your life.

This is also *not* your Asshat. Oh, sure, you *say* you'd never choose your Asshat as your Trusted Advisor, but you might! Here's how that might sound:

> "So, I'm embarking on a recovery program that will teach me how *not* to take your crap anymore.
>
> "See how strong and independent I am? See how I won't take your crap? Isn't that appealing?
>
> "I love myself enough to do this, even if that means things have to change between us. Doesn't that make you want to get rid of other women who aren't as confident and together as me, even though I'm really not and am just trying to trick you?"

So no, your Asshat can't be your Trusted Advisor.

This must be a *safe person* to share with, someone who listens and guides you from a place of non-judgmental compassion and practicality.

Who Your Trusted Advisor *Could* Be

If you're in a Twelve Step recovery group, a trusted advisor could be your sponsor, or you might choose an addiction professional, spiritual advisor, life coach, or private therapist.

Poolboys Can Be Pricey!!

Granted, some of these options cost money. And some may simply not work out for you.

But, I'm here to tell you there is *no better way* to spend your time, energy and money than on your mental, emotional and spiritual health.

Here's why:

If you're struggling emotionally, spiritually and mentally, there's a very good chance that you're self-medicating by spending your money on new dresses, trips you can't afford, drugs — both legal and illegal — alcohol, strippers, mayhaps pool boys.

And while spending your money that way is a lot more fun *in the moment*, over the long haul it just keeps you mired down in the same muck, possibly with a massive amount of debt and Suze Orman shaming you from her financial pulpit. You just *know* you don't want that!

Eventually you *will* find the right Trusted Advisor and you'll wake up one day wiping the last of the dysfunctional ooze off the bottom of your shoes.

I had three therapists over the course of 10 years.

* The first helped me grieve my childhood losses.
* The second was always late, seemed crazier than I was and did no good, but also no harm. I moved on from her after four months.
* The third helped me prepare to love my husband and toasted us front-and-center at our wedding.

I lost a little money on that second therapist, but I have absolutely no regrets.

So, surround yourself with people who'll support you to make better choices. And a great therapist, counselor or life coach can be a game changer.

Task B: Join a Twelve Step group – they're free!

I recommend this path for many reasons, but the most practical is its cost and convenience.

Meetings are available everywhere, at nearly every time of day or night.

You can attend as many as you like, and even get the support of a sponsor paying less than what it costs to buy a cup of coffee per meeting.

And recovery, especially when we're in crisis, needs to be part of our repertoire every single day.

When we're training for a marathon we run daily to reshape our muscles and strengthen our heart and lungs for the daunting task on race day.

When we begin recovery, weekly therapy and reading the odd self-help book will be helpful, but that isn't going to give you the radical, ongoing support you need for transformation.

You've got to engage with your fellow sufferers as frequently as possible in order to change long-standing compulsions.

What Worked for Me

When I hit rock bottom with Mister Cruelly Handsome, my therapist encouraged me to join the Al-Anon Twelve Step program and find a sponsor who could help me work the steps.

This suited my pocketbook given that I was a waitress with a few small acting gigs here and there.

At that time, I needed more than a once-a-week sanity pit stop. I needed an overhaul that required daily practice.

In the beginning, I averaged three meetings a week. But it's not uncommon for people starting recovery to attend 30 meetings in 30 days.

This shocks your system, replacing old patterns with new ones and building your mental health muscles daily.

But most importantly, Twelve Step meetings catapult you out of isolation. You have a built-in Mental Health Village to help forestall addiction relapse.

The Twelve Step programs aren't the only recovery programs available. I'm sure many organizations have their own platforms.

But you must be very careful in selecting one. You want to avoid, at all costs, Cults of Personality.

(Jim Jones, David Koresh and Bikram Yoga, "the alleged woman molester," come to mind.)

What I like most about the Twelve Step programs is that no *one* person is permanently in charge. Volunteers run the meetings and must rotate responsibilities every six months. There's little room for one person's ego and charisma to run amuck.

Twelve Step programs are also *not* evangelical. As mentioned, their motto for bringing in new members is "through attraction, not promotion."

Your Reservations

I know that nobody wants to sit down with a group of strangers and reveal their most embarrassing secrets.

No, No, I Looove Talking About My Secret Shame ...

... It's Right up There with Getting a Pap Smear!

Many of my clients are reluctant to go to meetings.

* Some are too embarrassed and ashamed.
* Some are doctors, lawyers or newscasters who don't want to broadcast their missteps and demons.
* Some are dyed-in-the-wool caretakers who worry that the people they meet in program will latch on to them and suck them dry.

If any of these concerns ring true for you, you should know that most Twelve Step programs offer <u>Phone Meetings</u>.

You can speak up if you like, or you can remain silent and just listen. This is often a safe way to see if Twelve Step recovery can work for you.

Whether you go to face-to-face meetings or phone meetings I suggest sharing when you become comfortable.

Once you do, I promise you'll find that admitting your pain to a group of people who have been there brings a great deal of healing, self-awareness and growth.

I felt I qualified for my program because there was alcoholism in my background. Even though Mister C.H. wasn't a drinker, he *did* have the some of the unpredictable behavior found in alcoholics.

When I sat down in my first Al-Anon meeting and listened, it was as if each person sitting in those chairs was living my life.

And even though I didn't like some of them — and I know some of them didn't like me — I learned that dysfunctional people, with the Twelve Steps, can help each other get better.

Have a look at the list below and determine *which* program seems most applicable to you:

* ACA - Adult Children of Alcoholics
* Codependents Anonymous — for People Seeking Healthy Relationships
* Co-Anon — For Friends and Family of Addicts.
* Al-Anon — For Friends and Family of Alcoholics
* SAA — Sex Addicts Anonymous
* SLAA - Sex and Love Addicts Anonymous

Whichever one you choose it's suggested that you attend at least six different meetings before you determine if Twelve Step programs aren't for you.

Remember that each meeting has its own level of recovery, tone, personality and vibe.

Rest assured, you'll feel welcomed and won't be pressured to participate, unless you want to.

(I want to make very clear that I'm not an employee of, or financial partner with any Twelve Step programs. I also have no vested interested in "selling God." I advocate the use of these programs because they changed my life.)

<u>Task C</u>: Get a Twelve-Step Sponsor

After listening and sharing for two months in the recovery group you like best, I suggest you ask someone to be your sponsor and start working the steps with them.

It's best to choose someone whose recovery you admire when you listen to them share. When we want to improve at tennis we play with a partner who is more advanced than we are.

The same holds true with emotional recovery. You want to learn from someone who's walked the walk and can lead the way.

While I learned a great deal about myself and made progress with my two excellent therapists, it was my Al-Anon sponsor who changed my life.

Her name was Joan. She was old enough to be my mother, had a Florence Henderson bob and sparkling blue eyes.

She was no-bullshit and as stubborn as a pitbull when it came to my recovery.

Joan was still married to her Alcoholic living in Ass-halla because she took her marital vows seriously. But she'd be damned if I went down the same path.

People who are still in difficult relationships can help you get out of yours. Strange, but true!

<u>How My Sponsor Single-Handedly Vanquished My Asshat</u>

One morning, apropos of nothing, Mister C.H. got dressed for work leaned over to kiss me goodbye and said:

"Shannon ... I've decided to move out. I know you want to get married and I think the only way I'll be able to do that is if I get enough space so I can back up and then run and *jump* into the marriage."

As drastic as that sounds, I believe Mister C.H. meant it. I believe he *wanted* to be capable of marrying me, but was panicking under pressure.

That didn't stop me from trying to convince him *not* to move out using my well-worn compelling tactics.

I tried seducing him into not moving out. I tried shaming and blaming him into not moving out. But to his credit, move out he did.

That's when Joan swooped in. She started calling me every single morning at 8 a.m.

She recognized that I was bargaining with myself about going backwards (to dating after five years) with Mister C.H. so she forced me to promise I wouldn't see, speak to, email or text him for one *entire* month.

Just thirty tiny, infinitesimal days! How hard could that be?

By day three I realized it was approximately as hard as holding back the tides.

"What's a month going to do?" I argued.

"Don't worry about that," Joan replied. "Just one month of complete radio silence and in that time, you and I are going to work the Twelve Steps like mad women."

As much as I wanted to recover, I still tried to push recovery away.

But Joan wore me down with prayers and Twelve Step literature until I grudgingly agreed to my sentence.

One month incommunicado and every morning Joan called and forced me to work the steps with the unremitting ferocity of a drill sergeant during boot camp.

There were mornings when the phone rang and I knew it was Joan that I refused to answer.

I didn't want to hear what she had to say.

I was too busy bargaining with myself about Mister C.H. *If I just saw him <u>once</u> to give his clothes back, that'd be okay, wouldn't it?*

But Joan was relentless. She'd keep calling throughout the day until I finally picked up. There were days I thought about taking out a restraining order against her.

Somehow a month passed. Then one day Mister C.H. arrived unexpectedly at the dog park where I was running our "practice children" aka dogs Shelby and Wyatt and Mister C.H. proposed marriage.

He didn't have a ring. I suspect the following day he would've changed his mind, but in that moment, he was sincere. A strange thing happened.

I saw, in my mind's eye, the face of a kind, loving man. He was an acquaintance at best. But I knew him to be conscientious and caring. We'd never flirted, let alone dated.

It was Michael. Three years later I married him. But I had no clue in that moment that *that* would happen in the future.

After one month incommunicado I wasn't happy yet, but I was definitely emotionally sober and finally had the strength and conviction to resist Mister C. H. and ask for another month to think about his proposal.

By the end of that month he'd found someone else. Which didn't matter, because I was *never* going back.

I believe without Joan's perseverance I would *not* be happily married to a loving man and I would *not* have my two beloved girls.

The bottom line is, we cannot heal from Asshat addiction alone. We need supporters. Even when we resent our supporters and want them to shut the hell up and leave us alone, we need 'em.

Recap of Exercise Three: Build Your Mental Health Village

Task A: Find a Trusted Advisor (therapist, spiritual advisor, life coach).

Task B: Join a Twelve Step group, they're free (or other support group that suits you).

Task C: Get a Twelve Step sponsor and start working the steps.

And remember the **"3 Cs of Recovery."**

1. Find your *Community*.
2. *Connect* with them face-to-face or by phone.
3. *Communicate* with them. Get real, be transparent and ask for help.

EXERCISE FOUR: ROLE MODELS SHAKEDOWN

Man, did I need me some role models!

In the thick of my last toxic relationship I'd begun dabbling in playwriting. One weekend I had the opportunity to stage and perform in one of my plays in a 99-seat theater in Hollywood.

I'd asked Mister C.H. to help by taking tickets and manning the lighting booth on opening night. Two years into our relationship I should've known better than to count on him.

So why did I decide to give him such an important task on such an important night?

I think Dr. Laura, author of the seminal '90s tome, *The Ten Stupid Things Women Do To Mess Up Their Lives,* would say I was suffering from "Stupid Devotion."

Which meant I was still *not* accepting the fact that Mister C.H. did not and never would have my back.

Yet, I continued trusting him with important things!

In this instance, I was supposed to swing by his apartment to pick him up at 6:30 pm for the 7:30 curtain call.

(It never even occurred to me that it might be nice if he picked *me* up instead!)

I figured this gave us enough time because the theater was geographically close.

But given Los Angeles traffic, it could take up to forty-five minutes to get there. This is why I was picking Mister C.H. up so early.

I didn't tell *him* that, however. Knowing his track record for keeping me waiting I didn't want him to think we had any lead-time.

(Manipulating him with dishonesty was how I participated in the Dance-of-Death.)

I arrived at his apartment at the designated hour to find him in the shower.

I tried to quell my annoyance, knowing that if he sniffed even a hint of disapproval he'd get mad at me for being mad at him and bail.

I sat on his futon, teeth clenched in frustration as I heard him take … the *longest shower known to man!*

It was like *The Mists of Avalon* up in there. The Lady of the Lake could've done the backstroke in that flooded bathroom

Damn That Six-Pack All to Hell!

The guy had never been cleaner when he finally emerged from that infernal shower.

Fifteen minutes had elapsed and now we *really* had to leave or we'd be late for curtain. But my guy was having difficulty figuring out what *outfit* to wear in the lighting booth.

Should he wear a turtleneck in case the theater was chilly? Or shorts and flip-flops in case it was hot?

I couldn't keep my irritation at bay and probably said something about not caring *what* he wore because we just needed to … *get the f#@k on the road!*

The next thing you know Mister C.H. is bailing on me, because, *if I wasn't going to appreciate his time, then maybe I didn't deserve it.*

My blood boiled. I imagined my fist smashing his big, fat, late face, but I knew, in doing so, I'd be out a lighting booth technician.

Also, who *knew* how long he'd banish me to Siberia? In the past he'd been able to ice me out for days!

I'll end the suspense. We *did* manage to get to the theater five minutes before curtain by having three near-accidents. And the show *did* go on.

But did I need the stress? No, I did not.

However, my inability to cut that guy loose was perplexing. I maintained my denial about the state of my relationship by telling myself:

"This is how relationships work. This is how *all* men are."

And I believed it, right up until I met my incredible relationship Role Models:

Carol and Brian

Carol was an actress who'd just finished a successful round of chemotherapy when she and I began rehearsing a play.

She wasn't supposed to drive, which is why her husband Brian drove her to and from rehearsal every night.

I must note here that Carol was bloated, pale and bald from all of the medicine coursing through her veins, while Brian was gorgeous and the picture of health.

I bring this up not to disparage Carol, but to highlight my belief that a woman had to be *physically perfect* to be loved. I'd learned that in my relationship with The Greek God.

I couldn't imagine someone loving me if I didn't look my most beautiful. Cancer was out of the question if I wanted to be loved.

Yet watching Carol and Brian, I saw she wasn't just loved minus her hair; she was *cherished.*

Brian brought little snacks, water and a warm sweater for Carol at evening rehearsals. He always dropped her off and picked her up on time. And he couldn't stop kissing her!

One night my mouth hit my chest when Carol asked Brian if he could draw her a "warm bath" after rehearsal, to which he responded, "Of course!"

Men actually drew women hot baths?

And Carol was equally loving. She always thanked Brian for his efforts and never had anything but wonderful stories to tell about him.

Say what?

> Oh my gosh, I love him soooo much!!

> I love her even more!!

What the hell was *this* all about? No complaining? No venting? No dumping about her crappy love partner?

Over the run of our show I watched Carol and Brian's relationship like a Ukrainian mobster looking for the Feds.

I just *knew* there had to be anger, resentment, unfulfilled needs and dominatrices somewhere under the surface!

But no! There was nothing like that; just fear that the cancer could return, which somehow made their love incandescent. They both understood how precious time was.

Seeing the scaffolding of a Real Love relationship was essential in helping me step away from my addiction to rakes and rogues.

I'd seen the Promised Land and, as God was my witness, I was going to get there!

A *Health Guidance* article says *this* about role models:

"Role models are highly important for us psychologically, help-ing to guide us to make important decisions that affect the outcome of our lives, and to help us find happiness."

Which is why *you* need to find *yours*.

Task A: Make a list of all the couples you know that have a rela-tionship you admire.

I'm not talking about phony, show-off relationships on social media feeds, but *real* relationships where the couple has each other's back in good times and *especially* in bad times.

Task B: Reach out to these couples and ask if you can talk to them about their relationship using the 3 Cs of Recovery: Community, Connection and Communication.

Don't be embarrassed to ask. People are usually flattered that you admire their union.

Miserable People Want You to Be Miserable! But, Happy People Want You to Be Happy!

When you reach out I want you to ask these five questions:

1. What made you fall in love with your partner?
2. What do you do to show each other how much you care?
3. How was your partner there for you during a difficult time?
4. How do you maintain trust in your relationship?
5. What are your shared values?

When we come from a background rife with relationship dysfunction we may have no idea what a healthy relationship looks like.

Role models can fill in the gaps and give us something concrete to aspire to.

<u>Recap of Exercise 4</u>: Role Models Shakedown

Task A: List the couples you know who have the relationship you admire.

Task B: Reach out to these couples and ask about their relationship, using the "3 Cs of Recovery" as your inspiration.

EXERCISE FIVE: INNER CHILD CHAMPION

learned about my "inner child" when I worked with my talented therapist Victor Morton Ph.d. Here's a brief description that I think perfectly encapsulates the term:

"[The] inner child is our childlike aspect. It includes all that we learned and experienced as children, before puberty.

"The inner child denotes a semi-independent entity subordinate to the waking conscious mind."

Tiny Buddha article, "7 Things Your Inner Child Needs to Hear You Say," explains why it's so important to understand, acknowledge, love and heal our inner child:

"Have you ever thought about why you can't move forward? Have you wondered why you sabotage yourself? Have you ever questioned why you so easily feel anxious, depressed, and self-critical? Inside each of us there's an inner child that was once wounded.

"To avoid the pain, we've tried to ignore that child, but she never goes away. Our inner child lives in our unconscious mind and influences how we make choices, respond to challenges, and live our lives."

My inner child felt abandoned when my mom's second marriage failed and she felt it best to send me to my dad while she tried to pull her life together.

My inner child interpreted this as a rejection so she became insecure and needy. She also felt unfairly criticized by my father – who struggled with his own self-criticism -- so she became a performance addict and people pleaser.

All those unconscious feelings wreaked havoc in just about every area of my adult life and had to be carefully, persistently and lovingly addressed.

Sienna's Story

My client Sienna came unexpectedly face-to-face with her inner child during a painful moment in her adult relationship with Patrick.

Sienna often blamed herself when things went wrong with Patrick.

His brand of chicanery was trifold; he often couldn't pay his portion of the rent, he came home late with no excuse and he demeaned Sienna in front of her friends.

Sienna responded with anger, but she always stuck around for more mistreatment. She referred to herself as an Angry Doormat.

It was true that Patrick could step all over her. But at least she'd *yell* at him while he was doing it.

Patrick was unfazed. It didn't matter how angry Sienna became, she couldn't scare that guy straight. He went right about his Ass-hellaciousness all the same.

Occasionally Patrick punished Sienna for her righteous anger by gathering most of his stuff and making a show of moving out of their apartment.

He'd usually return within a week, after Sienna begged and pleaded and apologized for being angry. But one night Sienna had a breakthrough.

She and Patrick had what had become a typical brouhaha about his staying out all night with his friends and Patrick decided to leave.

He was walking out the front door, carrying their rosewood coffee table as per usual, when Sienna angrily cried out, "I feel so used!"

This surprised her because she didn't realize until that moment that every time she went through the cycle of abuse with Patrick, he was draining her jet fuel.

Their cycle looked like this:

* Sienna catered to Patrick with food, love and sex.
* Patrick continued to disrespect Sienna by using her financially, being inconsistent and publicly critical.
* Sienna exploded and left.
* Then Sienna freaked out, apologized and went back for more.

What Was Different This Time?

Sienna had been angry at Pat many times before, and angry at herself for staying, but this time was different.

This time, after being in recovery for three months, Sienna was angry *for* herself. Specifically, **she was angry for her inner child.**

Sienna realized she'd abandoned her inner child over and over, the same way her dad — who left when she was three — had abandoned her during a bad divorce.

Listening to, loving and taking care of her inner child helped Sienna quit Pat for good. And you can learn to do the same thing.

Task A: Find a photograph of yourself as a child during a turbulent time.

My parents divorced when I was two-years-old. It was a revelation to see the difference in photos of me:

Before the Divorce   **After the Divorce**

Granted, that uncertain, somber look in my After photo may have reflected a child who just needed a good nap or had entered her Terrible Twos phase.

But when I see my toddler face I remember that little girl's confusion.

Placing those photos somewhere I could see them daily helped launch my "inner child" work.

So, find the photos from a time in your childhood when you may have been experiencing turbulence. Place them somewhere you can see them every single day.

Task B: Talk to that child out loud.

Tell her that you're working to become strong enough to parent and keep her safe.

Tell her that you see her, you love her and that she is beautiful and worthy of support, safety and respect.

Exercise compassion for this child. When it comes to recovery, the goal is "progress not perfection."

We tried to be perfect when we were children. Now we know that's a recipe for disaster. So be kind and patient with yourself.

Recap of Exercise Five: Inner Child Champion

Task A: Find a photograph of yourself taken during a turbulent time in your childhood. Place it somewhere you can see it every day.

Task B: Reassure that child out loud that you're becoming strong enough to parent her and keep her safe.

Bonus Task: Read John Bradshaw's book, *Homecoming: Reclaiming and Healing Your Inner Child.*

EXERCISE SIX: CONNECT WITH YOUR HIGHER POWER

was raised in a strict Christian religion, which didn't suit me. It made me suspicious of and annoyed by "God" and that guy Jesus.

As far as I was concerned I hadn't asked *anyone* to die for my sins and resented the possibility I might go to Hell for reading bodice rippers that made me want to have premarital sex.

I became agnostic and wore my agnosticism like a Girl Scout merit badge.

I threw the baby out with the bathwater, confusing Religion with Spirituality. They are two entirely different things.

Sometimes my parents had the missionaries show up at our house to convince me to be baptized. This was my inner monologue:

Through the steady, extended use of my rational brain I've decided I don't know if God exists and you can't make me! So missionaries -- gosh you're handsome and I'd like to sinfully make out with you -- get back on your bicycles and be gone!

So when I began working the Twelve Steps to circumvent my toxic relationship patterns, I found Step Two daunting.

I had to get humble enough to at least *entertain* the notion I could ask a Higher Power for help.

This led me to work Step Two in my Twelve Step program. Here's a reminder of that step from our reference page:

<u>Step Two</u>: *Came to Believe That a Power Greater Than Ourselves Could Restore Us to Sanity.*

I attempted to work this step by praying. This did not come naturally for me. My prayers sounded something like this:

Why am I praying to an empty room? No one is out there. I can hear my voice echo ...!

I wonder if I have any chocolate? I could just pause this prayer and go find chocolate ... (now eating chocolate) ... Oh, this is some good chocolate ... Focus, Shannon! Focus on praying to this empty room!

... I wonder what Mister C.H. is doing right now? He's probably dancing in a nude conga line at a Gentleman's bar ... my knees hurt in this position. Do I have to pray on my knees? Couldn't I stand or do it while stalking my boyfriend? ...

Also, I disliked the word "God." It was laden with guilt and shame for me.

I played with "Higher Power," but couldn't picture anybody. I had the same problem with "The Divine," "The Collective Unconscious," "The Universe."

I floundered. Then a particularly wise program friend gave me two simple tasks that utterly revolutionized my relationship with my Higher Power, which I'm going to offer you now.

Task A: Write down, in detail, what God is to you *right now*.

How does God *look* to you? Is God a "he" or a "she" or an "it?"

Does God love you unconditionally? Or think you're not living up to your potential? Or worse, making the world an even bigger mess than it already is?

Is there a God or just a Dirt Nap?

You get the picture. Don't judge your image; just write it down. This is what I wrote in my trusty Asshat Recovery Notebook that day:

"That word. 'God.' It already pisses me off and alienates me. It's like he's the Big Shot, the Big Guy. God!

"I have to schedule an appointment to see him. And then he only thinks about how annoying I am. How petty my little problems are. What a small person I am.

"Also, He's a He. My female self seems dirty, somehow, in his presence.

"My feelings of lust, fear and laziness disgust him. He gets angry when I don't use the gifts and abilities he's given me.

"I feel annoyed by God's expectations of me, of the burden of my potential – the one I'm not living up to.

"I feel God is sick of me. He doesn't like me. He doesn't know me. We have no bond. Me and God."

No wonder I sucked at praying when *this* God was my only option.

Task B: Write down what you *wish* your God could be if you could choose anything your heart desires. Leave out no detail.

There's a belief in Twelve Step rooms that people with high I.Q.s are hardest to help, because they're too smart for their own good.

They hate to ask for help, especially from some fictitious "Higher Power."

They tend to only have faith in their intellectual reasoning and are proudly married to "being right" all the time.

While I'm no genius, I was very skeptical about believing in a concocted, pseudo-God. But at this juncture I was miserable and humble enough to try anything.

I secretly hoped that God *did* exist.

Not the Old Testament God, full of brimstone and wrath, but one that might be a little more like Winnie-the-Pooh, cuddly and forgiving.

So I wrote this:

"God created the sunset for me to see, the purple, the pink, against the slate blue of the deep and beautiful ocean.

"He is constantly awed and pleased by all my new discoveries. He looks on me, his soft, feminine creation, with wonder and pride.

"God loves me every second of every minute of every day, even when I'm lazy or obsessing. God loves me when I'm good, bad, scared, hurt.

"He looks on and whispers words of encouragement. He knows that when the time is right I'll discover all I need to know, who I need to be.

"He forgives me for every mistake I've ever made. He forgives me for every bad thought I've ever had. He forgives me because he is Love.

"He's in my chest, near my heart, waiting patiently for me to know he loves me, he accepts me, he sees me, he hears me, he believes me, he is proud of me, my existence gives him joy.

"God is my father and my mother. He wants the world, the heavens, the stars, the moon for me."

By the time I wrote the last word, tears flowed freely down my face.

I knew, with absolute certainty that *this* was the Higher Power of *my own* understanding, and that, although I couldn't see him, God was real for me.

During my chaotic early years, I spent a large part of my summer with my maternal grandma, Ellen. She was as predictable as the sun rising.

During my stay, we'd say *The Lord's Prayer* together before bed. It was a ritual I loved since I didn't have many rituals in my primary homes.

Back then those simple prayers with my grandma made me certain God existed, and that angels sat on my shoulder keeping me safe.

But that ended when childhood did. Until this exercise brought God back to me. And when I continued to feel doubtful, I decided to "act as if" I had faith in a power greater than myself, until I did.

"Acting as If" Something Is True Is a Powerful Way of Making It So. This Can Also Be Referred to as the "Law of Attraction."

Equipped with this new definition of God, whom I decided to call my Higher Power after all, praying became more natural.

I complained a great deal to my HP about my situation and inability to change it, but I also mentioned that I was open to suggestions.

This felt a bit loony. How did I expect to receive this advice? In a telegram? Because I certainly didn't consider myself the kind of intuitive person who'd have a "deep knowing" that something was conveyed esoterically.

Still, I was trying not to be such a little bitch, so I told my Higher Power I was listening if s/he wanted to send some messages my way.

Then One Day Something Esoteric Happened

It was one of the more challenging moments in my relationship. Mister C.H. was breaking up with me.

Granted, as you may be noticing, this happened frequently, but *this* time he thought it best to drive me an hour up the Pacific Coast Highway to do it.

Which meant an hour drive back with a broken heart.

I was just contemplating that horrible fate as we sat on a frigid, mostly deserted beach on a winter day.

"I don't think our relationship is working ..." Mister C.H. was saying, when suddenly I had to pee like a camel.

My bladder seemed to be controlled by a force greater than my body.

"Hold that thought," I gasped then dashed off to the beach bathroom, praying as I went:

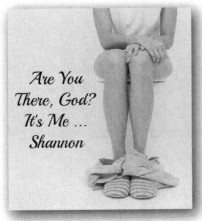

Are You There, God? It's Me ... Shannon

"Hey Higher Power, are you there? You probably aren't, but just please don't let Mister C.H. break up with me.

"Please soften his heart and make him realize that deep down he really loves me. And that he's frightened because of his childhood issues!"

When I entered the women's bathroom I was briefly distracted by how clean it was, since beach bathrooms tend to be disgusting.

I dashed into one of the stalls still praying for the salvation of my relationship when I realized this bathroom really *was* clean.

Because there wasn't even any graffiti on the walls. Nothing. Nada. Zipola. Except for *two small words* scratched into the wall by some kind of sharp object.

As I squatted on the toilet, the words were exactly at eye level: **No Future.**

WTHell?? Okay, I'd told my Higher Power that I was open to the messages and words around me.

Even so, I found myself barking aloud, "That's just a coincidence!"

"Coincidence is God's way of remaining anonymous."
-- Albert Einstein

But I knew, in my skeptical heart, that it was *indeed* a message meant for me from some realm my puny, codependent human brain couldn't fathom.

And it was *my* decision whether to take the advice or not.

I wasn't ready at that time to cut bait. But I could see, literally, the writing on the wall. And so I kept talking, praying and trying to develop a relationship with my Higher Power.

Task C: Connect and Communicate with the Higher Power of your understanding.

Prayer isn't the only viable route you can choose to connect with a power greater than yourself:

The God Box

A God Box is essentially any type of receptacle in which you can put little scraps of paper that you've written your worries, hopes and fears on.

By "handing" God your worries you allow him to work on your problems while you're sleeping, eating and reading lots of great recovery books.

This is the embodiment of the Twelve Step motto, "Let go and let God." You compartmentalize your problems so life can be lived.

For many of us the Box is God.

Meditation

My favorite simple description of meditation comes from Andy Puddicombe of *Headspace*. He says:

"Imagine a very clear blue sky. My guess is it feels pretty nice, right? All that space. But when you think about a sky which is … kind of a little dark, you don't naturally feel so good. Now the strange thing is, even on a very cloudy day the blue sky is still there, right?

"If you get on a plane and fly up through the clouds, the sky's still blue. It's just that we forget. We get so ... fixated by the clouds that we forget that there's actually still blue sky on the other side.

"This is a really useful analogy for meditation. Rather than trying to create a state of blue sky, a state of happiness and calm, it's more a question of setting up a deck chair in the backyard and just sitting back and waiting for the clouds to part."

Many people find they *do* feel connected to God or a Higher Power when they meditate. For them, the Blue Sky is God.

Yoga

This has been surprisingly effective at centering me, bringing me into the present moment and into my body.

Because yoga is meditation through movement, I highly recommend it for people who are too antsy to meditate.

It's also physically challenging and helps you focus on the life-giving power of breath. For some people, the Breath is God.

Emotional Health and Recovery Literature

The right literature can be incredibly helpful when it comes to forging conscious contact with a Higher Power.

My literature miracle occurred at 4 a.m. on a black, black Tuesday.

I couldn't sleep. I was turning 30 the next day and my life sucked.

My love life was in disrepair, even worse my "acting" career was so incredibly slow you couldn't even call it a hobby.

Living on a waitress's budget was a month-to-month crapshoot.

I'd been tossing and turning for hours when I began to feel tightness in my chest. My heart was kicking like a panicked donkey and I started to hyperventilate.

I wasn't exactly sure what was happening to my body and brain, but it felt physiological and entirely involuntary.

I didn't know what to do.

Should I call 911? Would my lousy health insurance cover it? What if there was nothing physically wrong with me and I was just a little or a lot crazy?

What I didn't know then was that I was having a full-blown panic attack.

Not knowing what else to do in the wee hours of the morn, I got out of bed, turned on the light and fought to keep the panic down.

Suddenly, out of the corner of my eye, I spotted the May edition of the *Daily Word*, an inspirational pamphlet of spiritual quotes and stories.

My ever-hopeful grandma had purchased me a lifetime subscription and amazingly this was one — the only one — that escaped the trash bin.

So, in the midst of this panic attack I spied the latest *Daily Word* and realized it had somehow found its way inside my solitary confinement cell.

I decided to read just one page. I felt ridiculous even *considering* a church crutch, but when you're having a panic attack … you *will* get religion.

I opened to the first page. There were only four words on it:

You Are Not Alone.

Oh, great. First, "No Future," and now *this*. I didn't feel like I had a choice. I got down on my knees and prayed. My prayer was simple. I just said one word. "Help."

Instantly I saw these words — as if in red neon — splashed across the black of my closed eyelids. "Don't go where you're not loved."

That's it.

"Don't go where you're not loved."

My heart stopped hammering. I could breathe. I was completely, emotionally sober and residing in my body, in the present moment.

I knew what the message meant. Right then and there, at 4 a.m. on the moldy carpet of my one-room studio apartment next to a seedy bar and a crack den, I quit my seven-year pursuit of an acting career.

I didn't know what I'd do *instead*.

But I knew that it wouldn't be acting. The relief that came from letting go of the dead dream was monumental.

That wasn't the only dead thing I needed to relinquish. I knew I needed to walk out of my debilitating relationship too.

But I was incredibly stubborn. It took more rock bottom moments before I was ready to work the Third Step in Twelve Step recovery:

Step Three: Made a Decision to Turn Our Will and Our Lives Over to the Care of Our Higher Power as We Understood Him.

That's a big one, especially for those of us who are terrified to relinquish control. This is where humility must gently enter.

Because as I've mentioned and personally learned, we can't fix our brain with our brain. We need the spiritual help of our Higher Power.

And if a "Higher Power" still feels uncomfortable, realize that this concept can be anything that works for *you*.

For some, their Higher Power is their Twelve Step group. For others, it's the blue sky, the God box, the breath.

For the cartoonist Callahan, who wrote a fabulous book called, *He Won't Get Far on Foot*, his Higher Power was a bottle cap he named Frank.

Don't confuse religion with spirituality, as I did. Be open to help from the HP of your understanding.

Recap of Exercise Six: **Connect with HP**

Task A: Write down, in detail, what God is to you right now.

Task B: Write down what you *wish* God could be if you could choose anything your heart desires. Leave out no detail.

Task C: Begin to connect and communicate with the Higher Power of your understanding through any means you deem effective.

* Prayer
* Meditation
* Yoga
* The God box
* Singing
* Dancing
* Laughing
* Suspending all cynicism
* Resigning from the debating committee

EXERCISE SEVEN: ADDRESS THE NINE ASSHAT RED FLAGS

In The Problem we focused on some of the red flags you may have noticed in your guy. Let's take a stroll down memory lane, shall we?

1. He comes on strong in the beginning, then cools off fast once you're hooked.
2. He's unreliable and inconsistent.
3. He actually *tells* you he's an Asshat.
4. He never wants to meet your friends or family.
5. If he *does* attend a family/friend event, he makes you pay by acting like a grumpy mute.
6. He is disliked and despised by your loved ones.
7. He uses the "C" word. (Criticism)
8. He says you're paranoid when you see signs he's cheating.
9. He cheats.

In this chapter, you'll address these red flags, move into deeper self-awareness and catapult into solution-mode. All of this comes courtesy of Step Four in the Twelve Steps.

Step Four: _We Made a Searching and Fearless Moral Inventory of Ourselves._

Taking self-inventory is critical in releasing traits and behaviors that keep us mired in The Problem

Let's look at red flags you may have ignored. Then we'll take action to peel that Denial Onion so we can grow, grow, grow!

Addressing Red Flag #1: He Comes on Strong in the Beginning Then Cools Off Fast Once You're Hooked.

I can't tell you how many of my clients feel utterly bamboozled when a man, who dove into them like an Olympian perform-ing a Half Gainer with a double-twist, suddenly withdraws.

What the Hell was that? Was it a bird? Was it a plane? Was it a freaking Asshat?

He may even abruptly end the relationship.

We codependents love to spend half of our lives trying to figure out _why_ he did this, which is a massive waste of time and an indicator we misplace responsibility.

So, let's just set him aside and focus on what you can control, which is you. Get out your Asshat Recovery Notebook and quill.

Task A: Write down all the emotions you felt when he unexpectedly withdrew or left.

Right after we had sex for the first time, Mister C.H. cancelled our very next date about an hour before he was supposed to arrive, with this heartfelt voice message:

"I can't make it tonight. Some shit came up."

These were my feelings:

* Embarrassment
* Hurt
* Anger
* Confusion
* Clinginess
* Shame

We'd only been dating a couple of weeks and the truth is I wasn't quite sure *how* I felt about him. So why did my feelings seem so much bigger than I thought they should?

I found the answer by looking into the past and so will you.

Task B: Write about a time early in your life, that you experienced the emotions your demoralizing situation has brought up.

How old were you? Who and what triggered these emotions? What were the circumstances?

As I reeled from Mister C.H.'s abrupt withdrawal I realized I'd felt these feelings many times before, especially with the Greek God in college.

But I went back much further. When I was 9-years-old my mom was in her crash-and-burn marriage, which sometimes included physical altercations. I came home one night to find her gone with no message, which was unusual.

The time grew later and I began to worry.

I walked around our neighborhood knocking on doors, growing frantic, fearing my stepfather had hurt her, or worse.

I thought it was my job to keep an eye on her, make sure she was safe. I did finally find her. She was at a neighbor's house laughing and talking over bottles of wine and couldn't understand why I was terrified and sobbing. I felt:

*   Embarrassment
*   Hurt
*   Anger
*   Confusion
*   Clinginess
*   Shame

When I came of dating age I began transferring the intense feelings I had for my beautiful, loving, yet unpredictable mom into my love relationships.

Understanding early emotional triggers teaches us it's not the man that's the real problem. He's just a symptom of damage done long ago.

In fact, we may have had these types of feelings with many *different* men.

The *real problem* is the cycle of emotional enmeshment we learned as children and fall into every time we fall in love.

Enmeshment

I was enmeshed with my mom growing up because I was afraid she'd die or leave and I tried to control and contain her to get my needs met.

It's that cycle of enmeshment we must eradicate. Just as child-Shannon tried to control her mom, adult Shannon tried to control her men.

When we step out of enmeshment, we stop giving away our power to the Asshat. Here's an explanation of enmeshment from -- Ross Rosenberg, M.Ed., LCPC, CADC, a national seminar trainer and psychotherapist.

What an Enmeshed Relationship Looks Like:

* You neglect other relationships because of a preoccupation or compulsion to be in the relationship.
* Your happiness or contentment relies on your relationship.
* Your self-esteem is contingent upon this relationship.
* When there's a conflict or disagreement in your relationship, you feel extreme anxiety or fear or a compulsion to fix the problem.
* When you're not around this person or can't talk to them, a feeling of loneliness pervades [your] psyche. Without that connection, the loneliness will increase to the point of creating irrational desires to reconnect.
* There's a symbiotic emotional connection. If they're angry, anxious or depressed, you're also angry, anxious or depressed. You absorb those feelings and are drawn to remediate them.

The next tasks are for Recovery Road-Warriors who've noticed:

Addressing Red Flag #2: He's Unreliable and Inconsistent

Let's say you want your guy to attend your nephew's bar mitzvah, here's what the inside of your head might sound like:

* *I'm going to be _really_ earnest and explain just how important this event is so he'll be there for me.*

* *Huh, that didn't work. He bailed at the last minute anyway.*
* *I'm going to pretend like the event isn't that important to me and that I don't care if he comes with me or not. I might even say I asked an old boyfriend to come with me in hopes my guy will get jealous and attend the event.*
* *Okay, that didn't work either. He unexpectedly took an overtime on the date of the event.*
* *I'm just going to cry. I'll cry day and night, right up to the event so that he'll come with me. That worked once.*
* *Drat! That didn't work either. Wtf?*

If these sound familiar, put down your handcuffs and taser and follow me to Step One in the Twelve-Step program.

Step One: We Admitted We Were Powerless Over Asshats, That Our Life Had Become Unmanageable.

There are many different ways to work this step. Here's what worked best for me.

Task C: Tabulate your behavior

You're going to list all the ways you've tried to exert power over your man and how those efforts have made your life unmanageable. Here are a few examples:

Power Play	Unmanageability
You pretend you're not hurt when he's inconsistent and unreliable.	You're furious with him and hate yourself for not standing up for yourself.

You have unprotected sex with him to be <u>so</u> good in bed he'll fall in love with you, even though you think his vow of monogamy is unreliable.	You expose yourself to sexually transmitted diseases. This self-abandonment fills you with shame and self-loathing.
You expect less and less of him while you give more and more.	This creates massive resentment that makes you finally explode. He then feels entitled to treat you poorly because he says *you* are the "Culprit of His Toxicity!"
You threaten to break up with him.	He calls your bluff. You try to leave but end up crawling back, which destroys your self-esteem.

Task D: Answer these questions:

* Did these attempts at power and control ever work?
* If so, for how long?
* When did things eventually revert to dysfunction?
* Would it be possible, and even a relief, for you to admit you are completely powerless over your man?
* What fears would that bring up? Write them down.
* When and where have you had these kinds of fears in your childhood?

While I know admitting we're powerless can seem terrifying, I promise you that over time:

You Can Find Power in Powerlessness!

This is because you've surrendered the Herculean endeavor of changing your man and have refocused your energy where it can work best — in changing yourself.

Task E: Make a list of productive things you _could've_ been doing with all the time you spent trying to change your man.

For example:

* I could've spent more time with friends and family.
* I could've taken that class in Alsatian cuisine.
* I could've taken up Pilates and Ping-Pong.
* I could've traveled to Quebec or Quito or simply the local Farmer's Market.
* I could've gotten myself into therapy or a strong support group.
* I could've read sanity-enhancing literature.
* I could've worked my program while remaining single for six months.
* I could've opened space for my perfect mate to appear.

Task F: Share your lists with your Mental Health Village, remembering: We're Only as Sick as Our Secrets.

Sharing the embarrassing lengths we'll go to in order to sustain a toxic relationship launches us out of isolation, gives us perspective and helps us make a game plan to manage our lives.

Addressing Red Flag #3: He Tells You He's an Asshat Right Up Front.

Sometimes you'll get the message, at the outset, loud and clear – _I'm telling you right now that I'm a mind-messing fuckwit!_

But you'll poo-poo the warning because you want what you want, so you're willing to ignore the Inner Voice of Reason that is screaming:

Disengage, Disengage, Disengage!

<u>His Warning</u>: Maybe he tells you up front he doesn't believe in monogamy.

<u>The Lie You Tell Yourself</u>: *Who says I'm looking for a monogamous relationship? I don't even know him. But, should I change my mind, I'm sure I could change his!*

<u>His Warning</u>: Maybe he tells you he's not looking for commitment or a relationship.

<u>The Lie You Tell Yourself</u>: *I don't really want a commitment either. I just want to have fun and hook up! It doesn't have to mean anything.*

<u>His Warning</u>: Maybe he tells you he likes to drink a lot.

<u>The Lie You Tell Yourself</u>: *That doesn't mean he's an alcoholic.*

<u>His Warning</u>: Maybe he says he doesn't ever want kids.

<u>The Lie You Tell Yourself</u>: *It's no big deal, because I don't know if I want kids or not; at least, not right now. Besides, if I end up liking him I can probably change his mind.*

And the beat goes on. Sometimes we have *no idea* how desperate we are for Love.

Desperate enough to lie and deny then regret it later when we're a gasping rainbow trout on his hook.

Not knowing *who* we are and *what* we need/want or *even worse*, lying to ourselves about who we are and what we need/want, is one of the main reasons we ignore this red flag.

A Success Story

Do you remember Helen from The Problem? She was the young woman who wanted to take a roll in the Seine with a sexy, drunken French ladies' man.

There was that pivotal moment in the car where he flat-out warned Helen that he had "nothing to offer."

Helen took a moment to consider this, rather than acting on impulse and diving into a situation that could end up a disastrous addiction.

She realized that even though she *thought* she only wanted a sexual adventure, there was a *good chance* she might develop feelings for the Frenchman and want more than that.

She'd done it in the past and realized she might be lying to herself. So Helen bid the Frenchman adieu and drove home alone.

Success!!

To Banish Asshats Be 100% Honest with Yourself About Who You Are, and What You Need

Sometimes we lie to ourselves so we can seem more appealing:

Oh no, I don't want marriage and babies, I'm happy to settle for the scraps you throw me because I'm independent and have no needs.

All this does is make us catnip for Asshats. We have to respect *our* wishes and ourselves first. Or no one else will.

<u>Task G</u>: Make a list of lies you've told yourself in order to get involved with a self-professed Asshat.

Some examples might be:

* My love will heal him.
* He's just my transition guy. I'm not really going to fall for him.
* He's been married three times. I'm sure the women were the problem.

Task H: Share the list with your Mental Health Village, including your Higher Power.

Sharing this list is *not* about bashing your guy. Remember, he's just a symptom of The Problem, which is getting stuck in emotional cycles of abuse.

Working these tasks is about *you* gaining deeper self-awareness.

As you continue taking stock of the behaviors, attitudes, lies and beliefs that are holding you back you can ask your Higher Power to remove them.

It can be embarrassing to admit the extent of our self-defeating behaviors, but uncovering them, owning them, sharing them and releasing them to our Higher Power is the crux of recovery.

Addressing Red Flags #4, #5 & #6:

* #4 He doesn't want to meet your friends and family.
* #5 If he does meet them, he makes you pay by acting like a grumpy mute.
* #6 Your friends and family really dislike/hate him.

Task I: List all the ways your guy has disappointed or embarrassed you in front of your friends and family.

For instance:

* He bailed at the last minute from your best friend's wedding where you were Maid of Honor and they'd already paid for his dinner! (Shannon sheepishly raises her hand.)
* He played *Call of Duty: Black Ops III* instead of engaging with your family while they ate Thanksgiving dinner.

* He drank too much grappa at your parents' Christmas party and knocked over the tree.
* He flirted with the cousin you hate (she gave you a wedgie when you were six and she was 10) at the family reunion in front of everybody.

This is for your own personal use. You're not supposed to lash your guy with all of his failings. It's not about him. *It's about you.*

It's to help you gauge the level of your self-esteem and the intensity of your addiction.

We must become aware of *who* we are and how deep our denial is before we can move forward.

Task J: List the ways you *wish* a partner would behave in social situations with your friends and family.

Some examples might be:

* He's eager to meet my friends and family because he knows they're important to me.
* He's warm and friendly, asking questions and engaging in conversation.
* He wants to make a good impression.
* I can trust him to handle himself without my badgering, assistance or intervention.
* My friends and family tell me later how much they really liked him and how happy they are for me to find such a gem.
* He looks forward to hanging with my people again soon.

The List of how you'd like your man to behave is even more valuable than the List of what you currently tolerate.

Because until we can *visualize* the way we want to be treated, it's easy for us to accept poor treatment.

We may even think that kind of behavior is normal and acceptable. It isn't. And guess what? Your man from your wish list *actually* exists! He's already been born and is walking around somewhere on planet earth just waiting to be your honey-man.

Honey-Man Definition

* He's loving. This includes hugs, kisses, snuggles, and even massages!
* He's generous. Meaning he attends events and is kind to those you love.
* He's giving. This includes helping cook, clean and bring home the bacon.
* He's consistent. There's no Dr. Jekyll/Mr. Hyde.
* He's an awesome dad.
* He's honest in a kind way.
* He doesn't have gin for breakfast.
* He thinks you're sexy and only has sex with you.

Be sure to share both lists with your Mental Health Village.

You might want to put the man on your wish list in your God Box as an affirmation. Or visualize him during yoga or meditation.

Visualization, goal setting, prayer and meditation are powerful tools when it comes to changing our lives.

Addressing Red Flag #7: He uses the "C" word. (Criticism)

What is it about we humans that makes us believe all the *bad* things people say about us, but doubt or look for an agenda every time someone gives us a compliment?

Women are especially bad at taking a compliment. If someone tells me I have beautiful eyes I might respond with, "No way, look at all of my laugh lines!"

If you're in an emotionally abusive relationship there's a very good chance you believe the criticism your partner slings your way.

So, I want to give you a lovely task that will be like a delicious sip of ice-cold water in the middle of a barren desert.

Task K: Ask 10 people you trust to tell you three positive adjectives that describe you.

You can email these folks, direct message them, text them, call them, send them a telegram or smoke signals. But you must ask at least 10 people! And give them a time frame for their response so it doesn't drift away.

I did this recently when I decided to re-brand my website.

I wasn't sure what direction I wanted to go in, so I put my question on Facebook to see if some of the adjectives would repeat and help me pick a direction.

It didn't prepare me for the sheer tsunami of love that came my way. Here are a few the adjectives my Facebook friends and family sent my way that they felt best described me:

"Bold," "Passionate," "Sassy," "Fierce," "Funny," "Playful," "Open-Hearted," "Enthusiastic," "Witty," "Authentic," "Compassionate," "Honest," "Generous" and, my favorite, "Willing to Talk About Uncomfortable Topics with Bravery."

What began as an exercise to discover my business brand ended in an exercise to accept My Good, to embrace all that love and come to believe it more than the critical voice left in my head from my toxic relationships.

This task might make you feel self-indulgent, embarrassed, nervous and afraid. Do it anyway, then sit back and accept Your Good.

This leaves us with the last two red flags:

Addressing Red Flags #8 and #9: He says you're paranoid when you see signs he's cheating. He cheats.

When we're little we have unerring intuition. Over time, when the people we love lie to us, we learn to distrust our instincts.

When we're in love with a philanderer who concocts elaborate lies to hide his infidelity and convinces us that our instincts are wrong, we become batshit crazy.

Here's a little snippet from my favorite film ever, *Terms of Endearment.*

Emma Horton (played by Debra Winger) is heavily pregnant when her husband, Flap, returns home from work *in the morning!*

This has been going on for some time and Emma's sure he's cheating. But Flap tells her she always gets paranoid when she's pregnant.

Emma feels like she's losing her mind and tries to get him to tell the truth once and for all.

Emma:

"Flap, if you are doing something and you're trying to make me feel crazy because I'm pregnant, then you may have sunk so low that you'll never recover.

"You may have just panicked, Flap, and in trying to save yourself, you've thrown out your character and principles. The only way to redeem yourself, and be the man God intended you to be, is to admit anything you might have been doing last night.

"Cuz if you don't do that, if you don't do that right now, you are a lost man. A shell, a bag of shit dust."

Man, I love that Emma. It's excruciating to discover infidelity. As much as we want to walk away, we might be too enmeshed to do it.

This is when you hit recovery hard, using any of these **Potpourri of Tasks:**

* Get super humble and ask for help from your Mental Health Village and the Higher Power of your own understanding.
* Get your fanny to as many Twelve Step meetings as you can. Al-Anon and CODA might work best.
* Work the Twelve Steps with a sponsor.
* Be kind to yourself. This means exercise, healthy foods, enough sleep.
* See a doctor if you can't sleep or are having panic attacks.
* Don't make threats you aren't prepared to carry out.
* Approach your recovery with self-compassion, self-compassion, self-compassion!

There may be a time you really, *really* want to believe your guy when he lies. During these times it's so important to remember:

Knowledge Is Power. Ignorance Is the <u>Opposite</u> of Bliss. Bliss antonyms: "Misery, Depression, Woe" -- the Thesaurus

<u>Caveat:</u> If you feel like you can't trust *anyone* you date to be faithful you may indeed be paranoid and should look into counseling to find out where the paranoia originates and if it's actually applicable to your current life.

Task L: **Before you ditch the relationship, you might say something like this to your man:**

"Some of your behavior makes it difficult for me to trust you. Trust isn't given. It's earned. If you want me to trust you, this is what I need ..."

Then tell him! While no one has the right to curtail any individual's privacy, if there's a trust issue you might simply ask for more transparency.

Some examples:

* You want to be "friends" on social media.
* You'd like to be invited out with any "new" friends of the opposite sex.
* You'd like more transparency when it comes to his computer and phone. (This doesn't mean you get to snoop of have passwords, but it might mean asking him not to go off to the bathroom and lock the door when he has a phone call.)
* You might ask for consistency and reliability in his behavior. Example: "Call when you say you will. Arrive when you say you will. Follow through on promises and commitments."

Your partner may or may not be willing to meet your needs.

The important thing is that you've had the courage to ask. Now you can make an informed decision about what to do with the relationship, depending on your man's response.

Recap of Exercise Seven: Address the Asshat Red Flags - Red Flag #1

Task A: List all the emotions you felt when your man unexpectedly withdrew or left.

Task B: Write about a time in your early life when you had these same emotions.

Understanding the source of our painful emotions is empowering, because we recognize that it's not the Asshat who is the real problem, he's just a symptom.

The *real* problem is the cycle of emotional enmeshment we fall into every time we fall in love.

Addressing Red Flag #2

Task C: Tabulate your controlling behaviors.
In one column, titled Power Play, list all the gambits you've tried in an effort control your man. In a second column, titled Unmanageability, list the ways these power plays made your life a mess.

Task D: Answer these questions about how the Power Plays worked out.

* Did these attempts at power and control ever work?
* If so, for how long?
* When did things eventually revert back to dysfunction?
* Would it be possible, and even a relief, for you to admit you are completely powerless over your man?
* What fears would that bring up? Write them down.
* When and where have you had these kinds of fears in your childhood?

Task E: List the productive things you could've been doing with all the time you spent trying to control or change your man.

Task F: Share your lists with your Mental Health Village, including your HP.

Addressing Red Flag #3

Task G: List the lies you've told yourself to get involved with a self-professed Asshat.

Task H: Share this list with your Mental Health Village.

Addressing Red Flags #4, #5 & #6

Task I: List the ways your guy has disappointed or embarrassed you in front of friend and family.

Task J: Write, in detail, the ways an ideal partner would behave in social situations with your friends and family.

Addressing Red Flag #7

Task K: Ask 10 people who have your back to tell you three positive adjectives that describe you.

Addressing Red Flags #8 & #9

Potpourri of Tasks: Hit Twelve Step recovery hard.

Task L: Before you ditch the relationship write down how your man could help you trust him, then tell him directly and honestly.

Make your decision about the relationship based on his response. (Which means his *actions*, not his *words*.)

Now let's get to the character traits we'd like to humbly implore our Higher Power to remove.

EXERCISE EIGHT: VANQUISH UNHELPFUL CHARACTER TRAITS

The next tasks address the **Ten Character Traits in Partners of Asshat.** To jog your memory, they are:

1. Family-of-Origin Dysfunction
2. An Intense Need for Love and Affection
3. Low Self-Esteem
4. An Inability to Set Healthy Boundaries
5. Codependent Personality Disorder
6. Insanity (i.e. You Behave Crazier than the Asshat!)
7. A God Complex
8. A Martyr Complex
9. Belief That Things Will Change If You Just Try Harder.
10. Compulsive Break-Up — Make Up Behavior

Let's start with:

Trait #1: Family-of-Origin Dysfunction

I doubt we can find a single family on the planet that isn't dysfunctional in some way. But there's a drastic sliding scale when it comes to the damage done to our emotional wellbeing as adults.

Task A: Answer these specific questions to measure the level of dysfunction in your family of origin:

* Do you feel guilty for standing up for yourself?
* Do you feel overly responsible for your Asshat?
* Are you afraid if you don't do things for your man whenever he wants that he'll leave you?
* Do you feel lonely and isolated?
* Do you constantly judge yourself and feel like you're falling short in love and life?

If any of these ring true, you've been affected by dysfunction.

Task B: Write down the coping mechanisms you developed as a child to survive/thrive in your home.

I'll give you examples.

Meredith's Story

Meredith's parents divorced when she was nine. It wasn't a good divorce ... for Meredith. Neither parent wanted custody. A judge forced them to share their daughter 50/50.

To combat her rejection, Meredith tried to capture her parents' love by developing the coping mechanisms of people-pleasing, success addiction and becoming a rescuer.

She helped her mom with her bipolar disorder and her dad with his alcoholism.

Meredith's coping mechanisms saw her through extreme dysfunction, but hardly set her up for a healthy adult relationship.

Task C: Describe how your childhood coping mechanisms have been destructive in your adult life.

Let's continue using Meredith's story as an example.

When she ended a long-term, painful relationship Meredith decided to quit taking birth control pills. She thought this would make her less likely to have casual sex and end up in another lousy love affair based solely on hormones.

The result? Three pregnancy scares in one year!

My initial advice to her was simple, "Start using birth control, yo!"

But sex is a sticky wicket for we mere mortals, and the impulse for sex had proved to be *too* great for Meredith those three times in the last year.

And because she hadn't *intended* to have sex, birth control was forgotten in the heat of the moment.

Meredith, an accomplished businesswoman in her late 20s, was behaving like an impulsive teenager. Why?

I asked her to answer this question in her journal: What *positive* outcome are you hoping for if you get pregnant?

Self-Destructive Behavior is Often Motivated by a Hidden Reward Lurking in Our Unconscious Mind.

Did Meredith hope the biological father would marry her if she became pregnant? Did she hope a baby would provide unconditional love?

Did she want to catch up to her friends who were getting married and having babies?

Meredith got to work writing it out. It was a question that needed to be peeled like the Denial Onion it was, going through layer after layer of her unconscious until she unearthed the truth.

We can't understand our motivations in an instant, but only through concerted self-examination. As I mentioned before, cuz I'm gonna tap it into your skull with my scribe hammer:

Journaling is an excellent tool for accessing the unconscious mind.

A few weeks later I received a phone call from Meredith. She'd had an epiphany.

"I think," Meredith murmured, her voice thick with tears, "that I still want my parents to take care of me. Because they never did!

"I've always been so capable, excelling in high school, getting through college on scholarships, landing a good job right away.

"But I realize I believe that if I screw up in a major way, like getting pregnant, they'll finally be there for me? Intellectually I know this isn't true, but I think my inner child is the one in charge and she wants her parents to take care of her."

This was a major break-through for Meredith.

She realized her inner child was rebelling against the coping mechanisms of people-pleasing, succeeding and rescuing. Her inner child wanted someone else to take care of *her* for once, so she was behaving irresponsibly.

Armed with this new insight Meredith decided to go back on birth control. And she's working diligently on re-parenting her inner child and growing her emotional/spiritual intelligence.

Your turn. Write down how your childhood coping mechanisms have been mucking up your adult life.

Take it in bite-sized chunks. One paragraph a day is often most manageable. Sometimes we're not emotionally prepared to write it all down in one go.

Task D: Share your work with your Mental Health Village and your HP.

The next tasks target those of us who have …

Trait #2: An Intense Need for Love and Affection

Task E: Which of the "Eight Signs of Love Addiction" apply to you?

1. Endlessly searching for *The One.*
2. Attracting troubled, addicted, abusive or emotionally unavailable partners.
3. Mistaking sex and romance for intimate love.
4. Using sex and/or love to mask loneliness or unhappiness.
5. Using seduction, sex or other schemes to attract or hold onto a partner.
6. Dressing seductively to attract attention, take risks or feel empowered.
7. Crossing sexual and relationship boundaries (i.e. engaging in a relationship with a married man or boss).
8. Constantly "falling in love" with strangers.

Task F: Write down how Love Addiction has wreaked havoc in your life.

My client Georgia was certain her boyfriend Ed was, at the very least, *thinking* about straying with other women, so she tried to be fantastic in bed in the hopes it would stop. (Love Addiction sign #5)

Each time Georgia used sex this way she abandoned herself, the way *she* felt abandoned in childhood.

This cut her self-worth off at the knees and further enmeshed her in the relationship, because she had *too much skin in the game* to admit defeat and walk away.

(In the financial world this is called "throwing more good money after bad.")

My client Lisa had an affair with her boss. When it ended, so did Lisa's job. (Love Addiction sign #7)

I suggest you take each one of the signs above and journal about if and how it applies to you.

Task G: Share your insights with your Mental Health Village.

Then humbly ask your Higher Power to make you aware of when you're self-sabotaging so you can course-correct. The following tasks address ...

Trait #3: Low Self-Esteem

If we've denied our true selves to please a parent, or rebelled to get their attention (even negative attention), we damage our self-esteem.

We may even grow to hate ourselves, which makes it nearly impossible to attract a healthy relationship.

Low self-esteem invariably takes root in our childhoods, but often we're not aware we have this character trait until we reach adulthood and all hell breaks loose.

There's Rosemary, for example, who sought her father's approval by bringing him "good grades like a dog fetching the newspaper?"

She had to find the source of her low self-esteem in order to stop people-pleasing in the present.

My client Heather did the polar-opposite of people-pleasing when it came to her highly critical father.

She rebelled against his rule by dropping out of high school her senior year to take a road trip with an older guy across country.

She even rebelled against her travel companion by hitchhiking every time he disagreed with her about anything.

In her late 20s, in a toxic relationship and incapable of holding down a job, Heather hit rock bottom.

She realized rebellion was doing the most damage to her by killing her self-esteem and throwing her life into chaos.

Task H: List the people whose approval you craved and didn't receive when you were a child.

This doesn't have to be a parent. It could be any authority figure from your childhood; including an older sibling.

Task I: Answer these questions:

* What did you do to try to get their attention? Did you people-please? Did you caretake? Did you provoke or rebel?
* How did these behaviors make you feel? Hung-over? Ashamed? Adrenalized? Elated? Defeated?

Describe those emotions.

Task J: Write down what you might've done if you *weren't* trying to please or provoke someone else.

Here are a few examples.

* Would you have quit the piano to follow your dream of playing softball?
* Would you have changed your college major from biochemistry to fine art?
* Would you have chosen a different job? Spouse? Life?
* Would you have said "no" to sex and drugs?

Address the Critical Inner Voices

Those of us with low self-esteem may have grown up under intense criticism. Often those critical voices emerge from our subconscious every time we try to improve our lives. It's important that we identify these voices when they appear so we can neutralize them.

Task K: Write down exactly what these critical voices say.

For example:

* *You're too demanding. No man will ever give you all the impossible things you want.*
* *You're too broken and neurotic to find someone who will love you as you are right now.*
* *You should be ashamed to want to get married and have kids. Why was there a Feminist Revolution if you're not even going to try to be like a man?*
* *You're a total screw-up. There's no way this will happen for you.*

Task L: Talk back to your critical voices.

Tell the voices why you deserve to feel safe and blessed with Real Love. These can become your affirmations. Here were some of mine.

* I'm a good person who deserves to be happy.
* I accept myself deeply and completely.
* I have confidence in my ability to do whatever I set my mind to.
* I love and accept myself unconditionally.
* I'm discovering more wonderful things about myself every day.
* I don't have to be perfect to be loved.

Although my responses sometimes felt forced, I kept at it. I was retraining my brain the way one trains to play First Violin at the Philharmonic to create astonishing, revolutionary self-love.

Task M: Repeat your affirmations every day when you wake up and before you go to bed.

Self-esteem grows by leaps and bounds when we replace the critical voices with positive, hopeful, loving voices.

In our childhoods, we had to adhere to these critical voices to survive. But we're adults now and we're in charge. So, we can build our self-esteem with consistent focus and effort.

The next set of tasks, are for those of us who have:

Trait #4: An Inability to Set Healthy Boundaries

When we're in a relationship with a boundary-pusher and we suffer from low self-esteem, people-pleasing, caretaking and that whole smorgasbord of obsequiousness, we can have no boundaries.

Do you remember Sandy who ended up in a ménage e trois? Hitting rock bottom in that relationship made Sandy so incredibly humble that she was willing to try *anything* to get some hard and fast boundaries.

Task N: Before you take any action for your Asshat, ask yourself two questions:

Question 1: Is it "For Fun and For Free?"

When your guy asks you to fold his laundry, lend him 50 bucks, take him to the airport, or have unprotected sex, stop and ask yourself: "Is it for fun and for free?"

This means that if you do this for him, you do *not* expect something in return. And to make sure you're not lying to yourself, ask:

Question 2: If you get *nothing* in return, will you be resentful?

If you answer "no" to the first question and "yes" to the second, you're learning to set healthy boundaries.

> **If Fulfilling your Guy's Request Isn't "For Fun and For Free" and It Will Make You Resentful, Just Say "No."**

My Twelve Step program taught me that "no" is a complete sentence. That was a tough one for me. My "no"s sounded like this:

"Um, oh, I don't think I can give you 50 bucks because I think my cat has pancreatitis, but maybe it'd be okay ... although I'm not sure I can afford it because I owe the bank $800 ... and I also need to pay my rent ... and and and ..."

I'd spend all my creative energy to justify saying "No" in a way that would hopefully make the Emotional Vampire decide to suck somewhere else and/or not break up with me.

Task O: Make "no" a complete sentence. Then write about the feelings that come up.

Just do it. Just say "no" the next time your guy wants you to give, give, give till you've got nothing left and then see what happens. Be like a scientist and take data. Notice what emotions come up.

* Do you feel guilty? Does this remind you of guilt you felt in your childhood?
* Do you feel angry for being put in the position of having to say "no?"
* Do you feel frightened? Are you worried that your guy will treat you badly, ice you out, cheat on you and/or leave you for it?

Now ask yourself, would you leave or cheat if your partner didn't pay your phone bill, finish typing your term paper, or give you Sex-on-Demand?

Task P: Share your findings with your Mental Health Village and your Higher Power.

In prayer, or the God Box, or during yoga and meditation, ask your Higher Power to help you recognize when you need to set a healthy boundary.

And if you do weaken when your guy pulls his puppy-dog face, use the **STOP technique** before you act. STOP stands for:

* Stop
* Take a Deep Breath

* Observe Your Thoughts and Feelings
* Proceed

Even in the heat of the moment we can stop and choose how to act, rather than react.

Trait #5: Codependent Personality Disorder

Melody Beattie, a pioneer in the field of codependency, tells us that, "codependents are reactionaries.

> "They overreact. They under-react. But rarely do they act. They react to the problems, pains, lives and behaviors of others."

Based on this quote I'd like to offer a task that illustrates the difference between *reacting* and *acting*.

Task Q: List the ways you *react* to your toxic guy and how these reactions are self-destructive. For instance:

Reacting	How This Is Self-Destructive
You think he's lying, so you admonish, shame, beg, plead, cajole and administer oral sex like a lie detector.	Loss of self-esteem.
He's late, so you get in your car and stalk all the places he told you he doesn't go to anymore (like his ex-girlfriend's house).	Stress, anxiety and shame about the compulsive behavior.

Task R: Write down what a *healthy* action might be instead.

* Making an outreach call to someone in your Mental Health Village to reason things out before you act.
* Praying and meditating.
* Noticing whether you are in HALT mode (Hungry, Angry, Lonely or Tired) and therefore vulnerable to overreacting.
* Attending a Twelve Step meeting, face-to-face or on the phone.
* Reading recovery literature and journaling.
* Beating the ever-loving crap out of a punching bag.

Another healthy action for codependence is practicing *detachment*.

What Is Detachment?

Melody Beattie says:

> "We cannot begin to work on ourselves, to live our own lives, feel our own feelings, and solve our own problems until we have detached from the object of our obsession."

This is what *unhealthy attachment* sounds like:

> *"I know what he should do! He should definitely stop drinking a Big Gulp of tequila in bed after losing his paycheck playing online Bingo."*

Man, the people we love can make a big mess we think we need to clean up. Except that we have *absolutely no power* to clean up anyone's mess but our own!

And part of cleaning up our own mess is learning to detach from the Asshat.

This doesn't mean we stick out a thumb and catch the next Greyhound to Memphis wearing nothing but a rhinestone tiara and a smile.

It also doesn't mean slamming down the phone and screaming that you're through. In Twelve Step rooms, there's a difference between detachment with an axe and *detachment with love*.

In detachment with love we begin reclaiming our own lives and sanity by allowing the Asshat to solve his own problems.

Joanne's Story

Joanne's ex-husband Caleb was a flake with their shared daughters. Not picking them up when he was supposed to. Forgetting gifts for birthdays or important events.

Joanne reacted by:

* Giving her ex a tongue-flaying about his Asshattery, which made him even more inconsistent and negligent.
* Making excuses for Caleb to their daughters when he forgot appointments, birthdays, graduations. This made the girls distrust their instincts.
* Continuing to rely on her ex to take care of the kids even though he'd let her down time and again.

For Joanne, *detaching with love* looked like this:

* She no longer covered for her ex with her daughters. Instead she explained that their dad's neglect wasn't their fault; he was incapable of behaving in a consistent, loving manner because of his own personal challenges.
* She set healthy boundaries by no longer relying on her ex in any way, especially when it came to child care.

Why Detaching May Help the Toxic Person

The core principle of *detaching with love* is that troubled people can't get better if we over-protect them. To learn from their mistakes, they must suffer the natural consequences of their behavior.

When Joanne covered for Caleb, she confused her daughters (kids smell lies like mice smell cheese) and enabled Caleb to avoid suffering the consequences of being a deadbeat dad.

Of course, *detachment with love* is very difficult when we're so hurt and angry.

We've got to go seriously Buddha with this, because *detaching with resentment* rarely works out … for us!

Detaching with resentment is usually driven by fear and anxiety, which cause us to react, not act.

We give ultimatums. We threaten. We withdraw in anger hoping that hurting the Asshat will get him to change.

When we *detach with love,* we have genuinely stopped trying to change him. Instead we focus on taking care of and loving ourselves.

If we're not sure whether we're "Detaching with Love or Resentment" we can take a moment to calm ourselves and check in.

We can ask ourselves whether we're detaching to hurt the toxic person in the hopes he'll change (NO!) or to take care of our needs and ourselves (YES!).

Trait #6: Insanity — You Behave Crazier Than the Asshat!

I'm going to tell you a very embarrassing personal story. Because none of the previous embarrassing personal stories will make you feel as superior to me as this one will. You're welcome.

It happened somewhere around my sophomore year of college during one of the down-cycling moments in my relationship with The Greek God.

By "down-cycling" I mean The GG was probably bored with me and either withdrawing or criticizing or having interactions with other women that made me feel insecure.

In this instance, I'd managed to get him to come to my parents' home with me for the weekend.

My parents were out of town so I imagined nights of reconnection and romance. Instead, he started playing pool with my sister's boyfriend and some other people we'd invited over.

After several hours of this I started to do everything in my power to tempt him from the pool table.

*   I flirted.
*   That didn't work.
*   I played a game with him.
*   That didn't work.
*   I asked him if he wanted to hang out with me.
*   "After I'm done playing pool" was his answer.
*   I asked if I'd done something to upset him.
*   "No" was his monosyllabic reply.
*   I tried to look fetching in the background.
*   He didn't fetch.

Finally, everyone left and we got into bed. He immediately turned his back to me, fell asleep and began snoring. What. The. *Fuck?*

I passive aggressively sniffled and sighed the whole night. I might have whimpered, too. But tomorrow is another day!! Just ask Scarlet O'Hara!

Except that he awoke the next day, peed, ate a bowl of Captain Crunch and started shooting pool with my sister's boyfriend all over again.

I saw every single shade of red. I marched over to him and shouted, "You are not playing any more pool!" and tried to wrestle the pool cue out of his hands!!

I remember kind of floating outside of my body, looking down at myself and thinking, *Wow, look at you! You are really pissed off!*

With a smirk, The Greek God won the pool cue wrestling match and bent over to line up his next shot.

That's when I slapped him in the face.

Yep. And I have to say it was quite satisfying. That is, until he picked me up by the shoulders, held me up to the ceiling and then dropped me.

It didn't hurt when I flumped on the ground, but it was pretty humiliating with my brother, sister and her boyfriend looking on.

So, did I quietly gather my dignity around me like a white mink stole when he grabbed his car keys and bolted?

Not exactly. I chased after him, grabbing him by the sleeve to stop him from getting into his car and peeling away like a house on fire.

I think; if I recall correctly, that I may have even grabbed the car door handle and run alongside the car for a block or two, until I had to let go or be dragged to the asphalt.

Can we say CAHRAZZZZZYYYY?

If the neighbors happened to be looking, who do you think they would've thought had issues? The guy driving away? Or the barefoot woman in her flannel pajamas shrieking as she tried to throw herself in front of his car?

Task 5: Write down all the times you've acted crazier than your toxic guy.

You're not going to do this with a self-shaming attitude. When an alcoholic drinks he might black out. When a codependent is rejected she might chase a car.

This task will give you clarity about which of your behaviors undermine your self-esteem.

Task T: Write down the results of your crazy behavior.

In my case, The Greek God didn't talk to me for a week.

I went into a shame cycle and drove by his house several times a day in the hopes we'd "run into each other," like I'd just *happened* to be in the neighborhood.

Task U: Write what you think an emotionally healthy person might have done in your shoes.

During my billiards-night-of-infamy, a healthier Shannon might have briefly pulled the Greek God aside and said, "I'd hoped this weekend would be a good time for us to reconnect, but I can see you're not interested. So, I'm going back to the dorms."

Granted, I was way too codependent for such sane behavior back then. But knowing what a healthy choice looks like would have been empowering.

Once you write your own healthy options, you can start praying and meditating about becoming the kind of person who can make the healthy choice and stand by it.

Trait #7: You have a God Complex

It isn't easy to know when we're playing God so I want to give you a *list of feelings* that indicate you're trying to heal, fix, control or shame your man.

1. Smugness:

When the Asshat comes crawling back after his scurrilous behavior, you might think: *I knew he'd eventually see I was right. I knew he couldn't manage without me. Now he'll give me everything I've been wanting all along. Mwhahahaha!*

That's smug.

2. Fear:

You worry that something terrible will happen to your guy without your love. *Maybe he'll drink and drive? Maybe he'll slash his wrists. Maybe, maybe, maybe ....*

Remember that your guy has his own spiritual path. And you may well be an impediment to him walking down it toward his own recovery.

3. Judgment:

Everyone you meet learns *exactly* what is wrong with your toxic guy. You itemize each crime and misdemeanor he's committed, being sure not to leave out any egregious detail.

You know things are reeeeaaallly bad when people politely excuse themselves when they see you coming, edging away from you as if you were an atomic chemical gone rogue.

And the Asshat frequently gets an earful of all his character defects, until he simply tunes you out or walks out and doesn't call for weeks.

As night must follow day, the God Complex is followed by:

Trait #8: The Martyr Complex

Your fear for his wellbeing shifts into fear that he's cheating. Your sense of righteousness shifts to apologies, begging and pleading when he gets fed up.

Pretty soon you are the most aggrieved martyr known to man second only to Job.

And around and around we go.

Task V: When you find yourself playing God or Martyr, detach from your toxic guy.

Call anyone and everyone in your Mental Health Village and put some elbow grease into working the Twelve Steps.

You may not be able to get rid of your own toxic feelings right away. But you can practice not reacting to them.

* If you feel smug, don't openly gloat and lord about.
* If you feel afraid, don't rescue your guy.
* If you feel judgmental, don't gossip, lead smear campaigns against your Asshat or engage in any other kind of crappy behavior.
* If you worry he's unfaithful, do not launch an espionage operation. Just work your recovery.

You can journal about your rotating God/Martyr Complexes and ask your Higher Power to remove them. Remember to practice an attitude of humility.

Trait #9: Belief That Things Will Get Better if We "Just Try Harder"

This one is painful because it makes us feel like we're not allowed to want anything. Because when we want something we try *really hard* to get it.

It's *fantastic* and important to want things. That's why we set goals, and specific ones at that.

But when we want Asshat Jack to stop drinking and wenching, propose to and marry us, be a great husband, son-in-law and dad, and we're willing to use every single ounce of jet fuel we have (and maybe borrow more from some unfortunate sucker) to *force this to happen* --- we are pushing the proverbial rock up a hill.

It will roll back down, crushing us in the process. We must drop the rock. To do this …

Task W: Be aware of when you're trying hard to change a person. Turn that focus back to yourself.

Look again at your specific goals, the ones that don't include manipulating someone else.

For me that meant telling myself and Mister C.H. the unvarnished truth. I wanted to get married within five years.

I didn't say I wanted to marry *him*. But I came clean and told him the truth.

As soon as I did our relationship shifted. He was on his way out, opening room for what I wanted to come in.

Trait #10: You're Stuck in Break Up/Make Up Cycles

Task X: Stop the cycles. Don't make any huge decisions for the first six months you're in recovery.

For Asshat lovers, leaving is usually about scaring our toxic guy into being who we want him to be. We're not really ready to leave. It's just another attempt at control and manipulation on our part.

And even in recovery we can get a bit cocky.

Oh, I'm gonna be soooo independent, emancipated and supported by my new badass Mental Health Village that my guy is either gonna shape up or I'm gonna ship him out!!

Yeah. That lasts right up until the moment he mopes, lies, withdraws, cheats or any variation thereof and we are right back to gnashing our teeth, moaning, begging, pleading and spying all over again.

Only this time we're even more embarrassed. The fact is, if you try to leave too soon you're subject to relapse.

So leave your relationship alone until you've got some recovery under your belt and your actions stem from your new emotional intelligence, your connection to a Higher Power, your belief in your values and your newfound self-love.

Not from your hidden agenda and spite. This is a spiritual journey.

And despite the fact I'm calling these guys Asshats to put a little distance between them and us, we still have to take the high road.

Recap of Exercise Eight: Vanquish Unhelpful Character Traits

Trait #1: Family-of-Origin Dysfunction

Task A: Answer these questions:

*   Do you feel guilty for standing up for yourself?
*   Do you feel overly responsible for your love target?
*   Are you afraid if you don't "perform" for your man that he'll leave you?
*   Do you feel lonely and isolated?
*   Do you constantly judge yourself and feel like you're falling short in love and life?

Task B: List the coping mechanisms you developed as a child to survive/thrive in your home.

Task C: Write down how these childhood coping mechanisms have been destructive in your adult life.

Task D: Share your work with your Mental Health Village and your HP.

Trait #2: Intense Need for Love and Affection

Task E: Answer which of the *Eight Signs of Love Addiction* apply to you.

Task F: List how each of these signs have wreaked havoc in your life.

Task G: Share your work with your Mental Health Village and HP.

Trait #3: Low Self-Esteem

Task H: List the people you sought approval from or rebelled against in childhood.

Task I: Answer these questions:

* What did you do to get their attention?
* How did these behaviors make you feel? Emotionally hung-over? Ashamed? Self-loathing? Victorious?

Task J: Write down what you might have done if you weren't busy performing or rebelling?

Task K: Write down the judgmental things your critical inner voice says about you.

Task L: List affirmations to counteract your critical inner voice.

Task M: Repeat your affirmations every day when you wake up and before you go to bed.

Trait #4: Inability to Set Healthy Boundaries

Task N: Before you take action for an Asshat ask yourself:

* Is it for Fun and for Free?
* Will I be resentful if I get nothing in return?

Task O: Make "no" a complete sentence, then write about the feelings that come up.

Task P: Share your findings with your Mental Health Village and your HP.

Trait #5: Codependent Personality Disorder

Task Q: List the ways you "react" to your toxic guy and how these reactions are self-destructive.

Task R: Write what "response" (healthy action) would look like instead.

Trait #6: You Behave Crazier Than the Asshat!

Task S: List the times you've acted crazier than your toxic chap.

Task T: Write down the results of your crazy behavior.

Task U: Write down what you think an emotionally healthy person might have done in your shoes.

Traits #7 and #8: You Have a God Complex and Martyr Complex

Task V: Identify your God Complex emotions. Then practice detachment from your provocative fellow.

Trait #9: Belief That Things Will Get Better if You "Just Try Harder."

Task W: Notice when you're trying hard to change a person then practice turning that focus back to yourself.

Trait #10: You're Stuck in Break Up/Make Up Cycles

Task X: Do not make any drastic decisions or changes for your first six months in recovery.

EXERCISE NINE: SALVAGE YOUR SELF

If you identified with **Six Ways Loving a Heartbreaker Changes Us** then you're ready to stop hurting and start healing.

Remember to approach this self-examination with compassion, not self-blame or criticism. Remind yourself frequently how brave you are to do this work.

Task A: List the ways you've changed since you became involved with a heartbreaker.

Perhaps you can relate to these examples:

*   I've neglected my family and lied to them about my love life.
*   I didn't go to my best friend's wedding because I felt like a loser and was jealous she has what I don't.
*   I missed out on career opportunities because I didn't want to travel where I couldn't keep an eye on my man.
*   I've become insecure, needy and compulsive, sneaking around and checking up on my boyfriend to see if he is cheating on me.
*   I've allowed disrespectful behavior like shaming and name-calling and come back for more.

Task B: Write down who you were *before* you got involved with your guy.

Examples might be:

* I ambitiously pursued my career.
* I got dressed up and went dancing with girlfriends every Saturday night.
* I worked out regularly and felt good about my body.
* I cooked beautiful meals and held potlucks at my house once a month.
* I slept well at night.

Write it all down. Then share it with your Mental Health Village and your Higher Power.

A Task to Reclaim Your Former Glory

If you feel you had no former glory, use this task to build your present glory one day at a time.

Task C: Start Time Recording.

Many businesses now use time-recording applications to learn how their employees spend their time. I suggest grabbing one of those apps to track the minutes, hours and days you spend drowning in codependency.

For example:

* How many minutes did you spend stalking your Lothario online?
* How far did you drive to see if his car was in front of his house?
* How much time was lost to mentally obsessing about him?

It can be incredibly startling to see how much of your life you're losing to your toxic relationship.

You don't need to beat yourself up about it. Remember, you have the disease of codependency and/or Love Addiction. But it's good information.

Once you have a baseline for how much time you're spending on the relationship, I want you to carve out time increments for self-care.

Let's say you drove an hour to your boyfriend's home and he ignored you. The following week, take that hour and schedule yoga.

* Or a meditation class.
* Or a Twelve Step meeting.
* Or something that will be a delicious bit of fun, like a salsa lesson or a trip to the beach with girlfriends.

Schedule in good stuff even if it feels forced. Even if it feels scary. Even if you think you don't deserve it.

Finally, keep the lists from Tasks A and B for future reference. That way you can track how your behavior changes — for the better.

I almost don't recognize the girl I used to be during my soul-crushing relationships.

I no longer feel or behave the way that girl did, because today I'm loved, respected, supported and even a little bit spoiled by the people in my life.

Toss His Bread Crumbs To the Ducks

If you're one of those who turn your guy's little crumbs into manna from heaven (Change #4) these tasks are for you.

Task D: List everything your man does that you consider a positive contribution to your relationship.

As you may recall, my client Caroline gushed when her Asshat left the world's smallest Christmas stocking on their mantle.

Be honest. What have you been giving your guy credit for? Leaving the toilet seat down? Putting his beer cans in recycling?

Be thorough. Write down at least 10 things.

Next think of a person or people with whom you have an uncomplicated, loving, and reciprocal relationship. Mine were:

The Hubba Hubba Girls

While I was not great at picking men, I was fabulous at picking girlfriends. I met the *Loves of my Life* (in friendship) when I was in fourth grade.

This was the year my mom went through her debilitating divorce and I moved in with my dad and stepmom.

I was a wreck.

First, I didn't fit in with my new family. Then when I finally did, I was dogged by the horrible sensation I was betraying my mom. I named this feeling, which was almost like a living person, "Divided Loyalties."

I felt like I was moving through the world with no skin on; like a sea creature who'd lost its shell.

This made everyday problems — from a mean kid on the playground to a bad hair day — seem insurmountable. Then I met Kelly in Mrs. Hibbard's class.

Kelly was a petite 4' 11." She was half-Mexican, half-Caucasian via Scotland. She was eagle-eyed, tigerishly intelligent, stubborn as a pitbull and fiercely selective in giving her friendship.

I was her polar-opposite, a people-pleaser who tried to be friends with everyone.

Years later, when I asked why she had chosen me, she said simply, "You were just so beautiful that I fell in love with you."

In doing so, she saved my life.

If you were going to be friends with Kelly, then you were also going to be friends with my bud Viv, a Latina with a spine of steel.

The "Hubba Hubba" Girls All Grown Up

They'd been sisters-by-choice since kindergarten. They finish each other's sentences to this day!

Kelly, Viv and I came to be known as "The Hubba Hubba Girls" because we'd whisper, like old-timey vaudeville performers, "hubba, hubba" when cute boys walked by.

We passed furtive notes back and forth about our most passionate crushes, giving them code names to avoid detection.

We shared our insights and sadness, and made each other laugh until we peed our pants. Forty years later, we still do.

So think about the people in your life who really have your back. And then …

Task E: Write down all the ways they contribute to your relationship.

Some examples:

* They make an effort to see you.
* They make you laugh and enjoy yourself.
* You can count on them.

* They support you in good times and bad.
* They want you to be happy.

Task F: Compare what your man does for you versus what your loving friends do for you.

These lists, placed alongside your "Perfect Mate" wish list, will clarify what *you* need in your romantic relationship and what you're not getting.

Be sure to share these lists with your Mental Health Village and your HP.

Recap of Exercise Nine: Salvage Yourself

Task A: Brainstorm all the ways you've changed since becoming involved with a heartbreaker.

Task B: Write down who you were pre-Asshat.

Task C: Record time spent pursuing your guy. Schedule in time for self-care and self-love, starting small and increasing slowly to move out of your comfort zone.

Throwing out the breadcrumbs ...

Task D: List everything your man does that you consider a positive contribution to your relationship.

Task E: List contributions from people who truly have your back (mine were The Hubba Hubba Girls).

Task F: Compare and share the two lists.

EXERCISE TEN: BECOME POWERLESS

If you relate to some of the **Seven Tactics I Tried to Change My Man ...** start taking your jet fuel back now!

Becoming your guy's mother, priest, parole officer or psychologist doesn't help him, *or you.*

Neither do Ouija boards, waterboarding or paying a thug to break his kneecaps.

If your motive is to get what you want, it won't work. The fact is, the Asshat was an Asshat before he ever laid eyes on you.

He is, and always has been, unpredictable and confusing, even to himself. And he must want to change for *himself*, not for you.

I must quote psychologist Steven Carter and author Julia Sokol's description of an Asshat sub-type they call the "commitmentphobe:"

"The commitmentphobic man is a man of two minds, each with a distinct and separate point of view. One wants to be in a good relationship with a woman who loves him. The other views a permanent relationship as a suffocating trap.

"To be involved with a commitmentphobic man is to enter into a strange world of double messages and contradictory behavior. He can't give a clear yes, and he can't say no. For every step forward does he take two back?"

Commitmentphobes Want You.
Then They Don't.
Then They Really, Really Do.
Until They Really, Really Don't.

Paola's Story

After two years of off-and-on dating, Paola managed to convince her love, Stephen, to move in with her.

She was thrilled that their relationship seemed to be moving in the right direction, which, for Paola, meant marriage and children.

One afternoon Paola and Stephen spent the day apartment hunting then returned to his apartment for what she thought was transcendent lovemaking.

He then dropped her at work for her evening nursing shift and said he'd be back at 11 to pick her up.

She waited curbside until 11:15. She texted and called. Nada.

She hoped nothing terrible had happened to Stephen, but she also kind of hoped something terrible *had* happened; like maybe broken fingers that made it impossible for him to answer his phone or to text her.

Because she knew all too well what this kind of behavior meant. He was freaking out and running away.

With a sinking feeling, around midnight, Paola called an Uber and went to Stephen's place. She found him sitting on the futon entwined with a woman she'd never seen before.

When Paola got angry, Stephen asked Paola, *not* the "other woman," to leave. WTF??

Paola was devastated. Not only by Stephan's infidelity, but the flagrant way he made *sure* she'd find out.

In retrospect, Paola realized that apartment hunting triggered Stephen's fear of commitment, which, for him equaled claustrophobia.

Picking up the other woman at a local bar (she found out later when she took him back) was his way of clawing out of the tomb commitment represented for him.

In her heart of hearts Paola knew she should've foreseen this event.

But there was nothing she could've done to stop it, except completely deny her wants and needs in the relationship.

And even if she had pretended *nothing* was enough for her, there was no guarantee Stephen wouldn't sabotage the relationship and flee for his life anyway.

Like Paola, there are plenty of smart, lovely women out there trying to get their needs met by forcing a situation. Then they're utterly confused by their Asshat's push-me/pull-you behavior.

One of the best ways to stop trying to change your man is to again apply Step One in Twelve Step recovery:

<u>Step One</u>: Admitted We Were Powerless over Others and That Our Lives Had Become Unmanageable.

Admitting you're powerless over your guy and refocusing your energy where you can actually make a difference is incredibly empowering.

I've found I come back to this step time and time again when I notice unmanageability cropping up in my life.

To embrace your powerlessness, try this:

Task A: List the ways in which you are powerless in your toxic relationship.

Here are some examples:

*   I am powerless over my guy's sudden, disruptive change of plans.
*   I am powerless over whether he'll return my phone calls or text messages.
*   I am powerless over whom he meets and sees when we're not together.
*   I am powerless over how he spends his money or time.
*   I am powerless over what kinds of drugs he puts in his body.
*   I am powerless over whether he'll cheat on me.
*   In short, I am powerless over him.

Take a long, hard look at your list. At first it might make you feel anxious, crazy and neurotic.

But stop and think about all the time and energy you spent trying to have power over these things. And if you somehow *did* manage to change his behavior once or twice, how long did it last?

Then take a moment to think about how it would feel to just give up, to just drop the oars and let go of control?

It's scary, of course. But can you begin to sense just the very first, faintest sensations of relief?

Can you? Because that is a feeling we want to invite more and more.

When anxiety grabs us by the throat, we can take pen to paper and remind ourselves of our powerlessness over any other being besides ourselves.

Task B: Follow Step Three of the Twelve Steps. Turn the list of things you'd like to control over to the care of your Higher Power.

I just heard you say, "Huh?" In truth, I don't know what that will look like for you. But I'll give you an example from my own life.

At the very end of my relationship with Mister C.H., I came into some unexpected cash and decided to visit the countries of my ancestors, Germany and the Czech Republic.

I really wanted my Casanova to come with me, worrying that if I left him to his own devices for 10 days he'd certainly cheat on me. But he declined.

So, I prayed to my Higher Power and asked if he could please make sure that my guy wasn't unfaithful while I was away. (Because I still hoped my HP was a short-order cook.)

Unsurprisingly, I didn't feel the usual "message received" from my HP.

Instead, as the trip grew closer I became more and more anxious. Then one day it occurred to me that I was powerless over my man's choices.

So I got on my knees and humbly asked my Higher Power to remove the shortcoming of "control" so I could detach from my toxic relationship while I was away.

I asked him to help me make the most of my trip. I asked for willingness to reconnect with myself; the self who loved to travel, meet new people and have adventures.

And guess what? My prayers were answered. I had the trip of a lifetime, with only one anxious, obsessive hour or two along the way.

When I got home I noticed my closest neighbors weren't willing to meet my eye. I finally confronted one of them who reluctantly admitted there had been an attractive woman coming and going from my home with Mister C.H. for most of the time I was gone.

And while he wouldn't admit it, my worries had been legitimate. Mister C.H. *had* been unfaithful to me while I was gone.

But he was incapable of stealing the pleasure of that trip from me. While I vaguely recall the good parts of my life with Mister C.H., I vividly recall that magical trip.

My ability to detach and enjoy my life regardless of my partner's behavior turned out to be the sea change I needed that helped my self-esteem take root and grow in earnest.

Task C: Make a daily commitment ... *to yourself.*

The Asshat isn't the only one suffering from commitmentphobia. Those of us who chase Asshats often run away from the people who actually *want* to commit to us.

Worse than that, we can't commit to ourselves.

We throw ourselves under the bus every single time our guy asks us to. Here are some fundamental things you can do instead of jumping through your guy's hoops:

* Pray and meditate, asking your Higher Power to remove the traits — such as low self-esteem, love and sex addiction, fear of commitment — that get in your way.
* Go to your support group once or twice a week.
* Work with a private professional.
* Work the Twelve Steps with a sponsor.
* Make a touchstone page in your journal in which you list the "living values" you want to invite into your life.
* Write, write, write.

There is a path out there for a lighter, happier, healthier life. Make a decision to do at least one thing *every single day* to walk that path.

If you can embrace your codependence as a disease, you can consider these actions the same as taking your daily medicine.

Recap of Exercise Ten: Become Powerless

Task A: Write down what you are powerless over in your toxic relationship.

Task B: Turn this over to the care of your Higher Power (Step Three of the Twelve Steps).

Task C: Make a daily commitment to your emotional and spiritual growth and healing.

EXERCISE ELEVEN: DETERMINE IF YOUR FEARS ARE REAL OR MEMOREX

If you related to the **Five Fears That Keep Us Paralyzed**, it's time to learn how to move on from emotional prison.

First we need to talk about how our childhood fears have shaped our brains, hence our adult choices.

When we were little and the adults we loved were flaky, distant, unpredictable, addicted and/or violent it affected the way our brain grew.

Research shows the brains of children raised in stressful environments are substantially different than the brains of children who were raised in stable, nurturing environments.

The Research

Dr. Charles A. Nelson of Boston Children's Hospital writes in his article *The Effects of Early Life Adversity on the Brain and Behavioral Development*:

> "Our genes supply the basic blueprint for brain development, but experience adjusts the underlying brain circuitry based on the unique environment in which each individual lives.

"(...) Early experience often exerts a particularly strong influence in shaping the functional properties of the immature brain."

Nelson goes on to say that painful life events early on can create long-term effects on the structure and the function of the brain.

Child Welfare Information Gateway's article, *Understanding the Effects of Maltreatment on Brain Development*, takes the topic a bit further, explaining in more detail how the growing brain is impacted:

"Toxic stress ... can have a variety of negative effects on children's brains. [It] can reduce the hippocampus's capacity to bring cortisol levels back to normal after a stressful event has occurred (Shonkoff, 2012).

"Cortisol (the stress hormone): Abnormal cortisol levels can have many negative effects. Lower cortisol levels can ... affect learning and socialization ... and lead to externalizing disorders (Bruce, Fisher, Pears, & Levine, 2009).

"Higher cortisol levels could harm cognitive processes, subdue immune and inflammatory reactions, or heighten the risk for affective disorders."

In short, toxic, dysfunctional and/or volatile environments, may have set up our brain structure for a perpetual state of fight-or-flight.

How This Might Manifest Itself

Shortly after the birth of our two daughters I developed a disease/inflammatory reaction, Irritable Bowel Syndrome. (An attractive ailment, I can assure you.)

I ended up losing about 20 pounds in two months because I stopped absorbing nutrients. I was in constant pain and had chronic insomnia and was struggling to be the kind of mother I wanted to be.

My gastroenterologist determined my disease was stress related. Off I ran to try ...

* Yoga. That didn't work, but I did get more bendy.
* Homeopathy. That didn't work, but my mouth was frequently full of what seemed to be dissolving sugar tablets (yum).
* Naturopathy. Nope. It *did* give me a rash, however.
* Meditation. *You* try sitting for an hour on an inflamed ass.
* Acupuncture. My chi resisted.
* Hypnotherapy. I paid the hypnotherapist $150 an hour, and *he* fired *me*! He said I was too anxious to hypnotize. Sigh.

I became more stressed out trying *not* to be stressed out! Finally, my gastroenterologist sent me to a psycho-pharmacologist.

I was mortified. *Hadn't all my years in therapy and recovery helped me at all? Did I really need to see a shrink with a pharmacology degree?*

Apparently, I did.

Within five minutes of hearing my childhood story she informed me I was suffering from post-traumatic stress disorder. The neural pathways in my brain were probably over-producing cortisol and I needed meds.

"Why now?" I asked. "I no longer keep the company of Asshats. I have a wonderful husband and two amazing kids. Shouldn't I be *less* stressed out?"

"What is your greatest fear about motherhood?" she asked.

I replied without thinking, "That I won't be able to take care of my children the way my mom wasn't able to finish the job of taking care of me."

Wow. I did *not* see that one coming. The realization was followed by a flood of tears.

This was a deep, subconscious fear that was triggering vast amounts of cortisol that I couldn't switch off like a light.

I didn't want to take anti-depressants. Doing so made me feel like a big fat failure. But three months into taking anti-depressants my disease went into remission, I was able to sleep and actually enjoy being the mommy of two beautiful, rambunctious, funny, dear daughters.

So, if you're suffering from perpetual fight-or-flight or just a constant level of anxiety produced from fluctuating cortisol levels, I highly recommend talking to your doctor about options.

It's difficult to fight our emotional triggers and fears even with the most supple, solid, beautiful brain in the world, let alone with our sweet, dear, imperfectly formed brain; in which case the miracles of modern medicine can help.

Again, these findings dovetail with the idea that codependency is a disease.

It *is* beyond our control. We *cannot* fix our brain with our brain. We need to accept our limits and find medical, as well as spiritual/emotional guidance.

In the meantime, let's determine what your fears are and whether they are "Real or Memorex."

Task A: List the fears you have about leaving your toxic relationship.

First, see if you relate to any of the fears specific to these personality types described by author Kimberly Key *(Psychology Today)*:

The Caretaker

"Caretakers ... crave intimacy and connection and work endlessly to take care of others—often to the neglect of their own health. Their underlying fear is of being unloved ... or not accepted for themselves alone, so they risk trying to change themselves in order to please others."

The Loyalist

"Loyalists seek the very thing they provide – loyalty. They desperately want security and support. Their underlying fear is not having the support ... they need and not being able to make it on their own."

Task B: List the positive things that *could* happen if you walked through your fears and left the toxic relationship.

Putting goals on paper sets into motion fundamental change in our unconscious brain. Here is my list of fears at the time, and beneath those, the positive outcome that *actually* happened when I walked through them:

Fear: If I leave my toxic imbroglio, no one better will want me.
Positive Outcome: I met and married my best friend after leaving my ex.
Fear: If I don't stay with my guy I might *never* meet a man soon enough to have children.
Positive Outcome: I'm raising two daughters in a drama-free, stable, loving home.
Fear: My man will crash and burn without me.
His Outcome: Within days he had a new girlfriend.

Fear: He'll give the next girl everything he didn't give me.

Positive Outcome: I was so happy in my new relationship that I genuinely didn't *care* if he was better to the next woman who came along.

In fact, a strange thing happened. About two years after we broke up I ran into Mister C.H. outside a restaurant where he was chatting up a gorgeous, tall drink of Brunette.

I tried to slip by undetected, but he spotted me.

He made sure to introduce me to the Beauty. I realized, in shaking her hand and saying, "Nice to meet you," that I sounded like a doctor meeting a patient who is terminal, that's how concerned I was for her.

Even more surprising, I was so indifferent to Mister C.H. that I forgot to tell him *I* was getting married in two weeks!

Fears can be big and scary, but nine times out of 10 they'll never come to pass. So, in dealing with your fears …

Task C: Make each "Fear" a person. (Or a zombie!)

Your fears might not ever completely go away.

But you *can* create distance from them by objectifying them. You can even doodle caricatures to represent them.

Greet them when they come along and explain that you plan to take action anyway, even if they tag along. Then:

Task D: List the ways in which you hide behind your fears.

For some of us there's a payoff in keeping the fear flames burning. If we hang onto *fear of rejection,* for instance, we can avoid the pain of risking failure in work, life and love.

But we also end up living a stagnant, tiny life that keeps us in a state of low-grade pain and self-loathing.

If we hang onto the *fear of success,* we might avoid the pain of people judging and envying us, but then we live with the consequences of abandoning ourselves to please others.

Task E: Work Step Six in the Twelve Step program.

Step Six: Were Entirely Ready to Have Our Higher Power Remove All These Defects of Character.

This one seems like a no-brainer. Who wants defects of character? But if we lose them, we fear we might also lose our guy.

Controlling, manipulating, self-abandonment, obsessing were some of the tools I used to keep my guy in line.

So, doing Tasks A-C gets us "ready" to *first,* have our Higher Power remove our fears (or if that's not possible, help us walk through them) so that *second,* we can be "entirely ready" to let go of our defects of character.

Task F: Work Step Seven in the 12-step program.

Step Seven: Humbly Asked Our Higher Power to Remove Our Shortcomings

You can use prayer, meditation, retreats or literature to connect and communicate with your Higher Power.

Or you can take your list of fears and codependent behaviors and burn them to a crisp.

There are as many ways to work the Seventh Step as there are people on the planet. Find the one that works for you and go for it!

A Few Awesome Quotes About Fear and Courage

"Courage is not the absence of fear, but rather the judgment that something else is more important than fear." – Ambrose Redmoon, *Beatnik*

"Courage is being afraid, but going on anyhow." – Dan Rather, news anchor, *CBS Evening News, gentleman*

"Courage is fear that has said its prayers." – Dorothy Bernard, *silent film actress, temptress.*

Recap of Exercise Eleven: Determine If Your Fears Are Real or Memorex

Task A: Write down every fear you have about leaving your toxic relationship.

Task B: List all the positive outcomes that *could* happen if you left the toxic relationship.

Task C: Make each "fear" a character you can talk back to, preferably aloud.

Example: "Hello Dolores aka Fear-That-I'll-Always-Be-Alone. Already this is a lie because I've gone out and built my Mental Health Village. I feel confident that the Higher Power of my own understanding has better plans for me than I could ever imagine for myself, and that will include abundance and love."

Task D: List the fears and codependent behaviors you hide behind and what you think they're protecting you from.

Tasks E and F: Work Steps Six and Seven in the Twelve Step program to vanquish them.

EXERCISE TWELVE: FOLLOW THIS "DATING ROAD MAP" TO INVITE REAL LOVE

How much easier would it be to nip our Love Addiction in the bud if we never got involved with an Asshat in the first place?

A Dating Road Map can set you up for success.

When we've had a habit of choosing one toxic Lothario after the next, the person we don't trust anymore *is ourselves.*

It's devastating to find out someone we *think* we love is untrustworthy, but it's equally distressing to feel like we can't trust ourselves.

So follow these dating rules in order to have your own back. Cuz if *you* don't do it, no one else will.

Dating Rule #1: Don't Lie to Yourself About Who You Are and What You Want.

I was proud of my client Helen, who bypassed the temptation of a torrid encounter with the sexy, sodden Frenchman who had "nothing to give."

She woman-ed up and got honest with herself, admitting she *might* be looking for more than a roll in the hay.

When It Comes to Dating, Sex Can Convince You You're "Falling in Love." (Which Sounds Like an Unexpected Accident.)

When you meet a person who floats your boat, be clear about what you want and take a wait-and-see approach as you get to know your love interest.

Does he want what *you* want? If he *doesn't* you could be in for some heartache.

For many years I told my ex that I wasn't looking for marriage and babies. I even convinced *myself* I didn't want marriage and babies for three reasons.

First: I interpreted wanting marriage and babies as weak, dependent and antithetical to Feminism with a capital "F."

Second: I was a child of divorce many times over and had developed a cynical attitude toward marriage in order to avoid the disappointment and despair I'd encounter if it ultimately failed.

Third: I suppressed my desire to marry, because I was codependent and enmeshed with Mister C.H. and knew he absolutely did NOT want the responsibilities of a wife and children.

I Was Afraid He'd Leave Me If I Admitted My Desires.

My five-year relationship would've been *much* shorter (if it had even gotten off the ground at all) had I written my "Perfect Mate" list *before* I was hooked.

It would've helped me get self-clarity from the get go. A few examples of what I would've <u>consciously</u> known before our first date:

I want a partner I can count on.

I was used to rescuing my boyfriends while *they* often pulled away or disappeared, especially if I voiced needs.

Instead of doing that, I would've attracted a man who'd be a strong support so that all the heavy lifting in our relationship wouldn't be left to me.

I want a partner who respects me.

It was clear that my guy had absolutely *no* respect for me; not for my feelings, my safety and especially not my time.

I'd occasionally go all Aretha Franklin on him, demanding R-E-S-P-E-C-T. But I'd struggle to maintain self-respect by setting healthy boundaries.

Trying to ensure I was respected felt like putting my finger into a disintegrating dam to keep the zillion tons of water (aka disrespect) from bursting out to destroy and drown everything in its wake.

I Was Exhausted Having to Do So Much Work Just to Get Someone to Be Nice to Me.

Instead, I would've attracted a person whose default was "treat others as you'd like to be treated."

I didn't want to have to *train* a man to treat me respectfully then maintain constant vigilance.

I want a partner who makes me laugh and thinks I'm funny.

Oh, Laughter, you Beauty, how I missed you.

I loved to laugh with friends and co-workers. I thought having that in a relationship would just be icing on the cake.

And no matter how funny a guy is; it's hard to laugh when all he does is make you cry.

<u>Dating Rule #2</u>: Know that you are lovable enough, beautiful enough and worthy enough to be treated with respect.

There are times I accidentally catch a glimpse of myself in a mirror or a storefront window and think, *Who the hell is that woman with the massive chin and no lips? Ack.*

There are other times that I really can't stand my personality and characteristics.

* Why must I always need to be the center of attention?
* Why can't I be a little more discreet instead of blabbing all my embarrassing secrets to anyone who will listen?
* How can my husband love someone who obsesses about her tummy size all the time?
* I hate myself for not loving myself more!

We *all* have moments of self-loathing. Some of us have days of self-loathing, others months and *years* of self-loathing.

None of us had perfect parents who only reflected love, joy and approval every time they looked into our bonny eyes.

So how do we come to know, in our very bones, that we are lovable enough, beautiful enough, talented enough and worthy enough to be treated with respect?

Here are some ideas that worked for me and have helped so many of my clients.

<u>Task A</u>: Go where the Real Love is.

Hang out with people who accept you as you are. They could be your co-workers. Your poker night buddies. Your version of the Hubba Hubba Girls. And remember that your Twelve Step group will *always* love you as you are

Learn to recognize:

* People who want you to play small.
* People who make you feel bad about yourself.
* People who drain all your jet fuel.

These rules can be applied to our families-of-origin as well.

We learned a lot of our dysfunctional information at home. Often we're lucky and our parents grow up with us, allowing us to have happy, healthy relationships with them in our adulthood.

But if they continue to heap abuse upon us, it may be time for a long hiatus. At least until we learn to set healthy limits with them, too.

Task B: Use your affirmations

By now you've got a list of affirmations at your disposal, but let's find out why affirmations are so powerful. Relationship specialist and author Eve Hogan says *this* in *Spirituality and Health*:

"When you say an affirmation over and over ... it sends a very clear message to your [brain] that this is important to you.

"[Your brain] gets busy noticing ways to help you achieve your goals. If ideal weight is your emphasis, you will suddenly begin to see every gym and weight loss product.

"If money is your goal, investment and earning opportunities will move to the forefront of your awareness. In essence, the affirmation can kick your creativity into high gear."

Escher adds that if the affirmation is at a "higher vibration" than what we perceive as true, an uncomfortable tension will emerge.

Let's say my affirmation is, "I'm in a loving, healthy romantic relationship that supports me and helps me soar." In reality, I'm still living in Asshat Central. How do I get rid of the tension this creates?

Escher writes, "One [way] is to stop saying the affirmation; the other is to raise the bar on reality by making the affirmation and reality match."

In other words, you let go of the unhealthy in order to invite the affirmation to manifest.

Here's the funny thing. Once you start saying your affirmations *out loud*, you actually begin to *believe* them.

And once you begin to believe something? Let me tell you, your jets are on *fire!*

You are vibrating at an entirely different frequency and your life will *absolutely* begin to change in ways you could never have imagined possible.

So, write your affirmations and say them daily. Even when you don't mean it. Do it anyway.

Dating Rule #3: Avoid the "Familiar" if you come from a painfully dysfunctional home.

Of course I was attracted to handsome men who had a coterie of beautiful women surrounding them. They were skirt-chasers like my stepfather, Trent.

So when it came to dating, post-Asshat, I had to be like George Costanza from TV classic, *Seinfeld* and "Do the Opposite!"

George, a dyed-in-the-wool loser and misanthrope, found he succeeded brilliantly with work and women if he simply thought about what he would *normally* do … and then did the exact opposite.

In Twelve Step recovery, they call this "Contrary Action." (Yes, it's a real thing!!)

Example:

* <u>My Normal</u>: Find a man attractive and fall into bed.
* <u>My Opposite</u>: Get to *know* a man as a friend first and spend several weeks deciding whether to become lovers.

Which leads me to:

<u>Dating Rule #4</u>: Do *not*, under any circumstances, allow your sexual organs to choose a long-term relationship.

Just don't do it!!! There's a reason some cultures still insist upon chaperones and arranged marriages.

They don't trust vaginas to make good choices.

My vagina can walk into a room, instinctively find the biggest Asshat there and pounce.

I blame her for tying me down *ten years* with my two toxic men.

The Vagina Monologues

My VajayLaw says:

"Sweet Mother of all that's Holy, who is that glowering, brooding, tall, muscular, tattooed man slinging back a tequila shooter while scanning the bar like a jaguar seeking prey?

"He looks like maybe he just got out of Rikers penitentiary for armed robbery. Or just rolled out of bed with a harem of

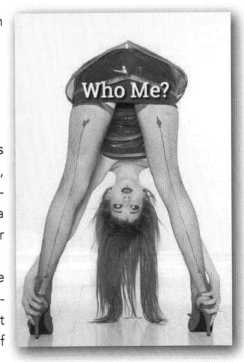
Who Me?

Kardashians. Or like he's that *Wolf of Wall Street* guy who bathed in dirty money and cocaine.

"I don't really care because all I know is I want him! And I want him bad.

"I don't care if he breaks my owner's heart. I'm a vagina and I'm all about me, me, me! Orgasms and pheromones trump common sense 100% of the time!"

Freaking vaginas and orgasms, man!

By the time I met my husband, the honey man, I didn't trust my vagina anymore. True to form, she gave him the cold shoulder.

She didn't find him intoxicating because he was reliable, kind, conscientious, a gentleman and he wasn't swarthy.

The pleasant irony is that in my Asshat relationships the sex got worse and worse. My sex life with my husband, however, has gotten better and better.

I had to reprogram my vagina, which was a challenge, but so worth it.

So please know, I'm not the Morality Police. Under the right circumstances sex is a gift. But we must be practical.

For many of us sex is the connective tissue in our relationships, both the good ones and, unfortunately the Asshat-tastic ones.

To see if you confuse Sex and Real Love, ask yourself these questions from the Sex and Love Addiction Twelve Step program:

SLAA Questions

1. Do you get "high" from sex and/or romance? Do you crash?
2. Do you feel like a lifeless puppet unless there is someone around with whom you can flirt?
3. Do you feel that you're not "really alive" unless you are with your sexual/ romantic partner?
4. Do you feel entitled to sex? (i.e. "Well *she* has sex with whoever she wants and *she's* not miserable so why can't I?!")

5. Do you find yourself flirting or sexualizing with someone even if you do not mean to?

There are 35 other questions listed on the SLAA site if you'd like to pop over and look at the rest.

Task C: If you answer "yes" to some of the questions above, describe how they manifest in your life.

For example: You might answer Question #4 (Do You Feel Entitled to Sex?) like this:

> "I'm entitled to sex because we're post-sexual revolution and women should be allowed to have sex just like men. With as many partners as we want, any time we want. It would be undermining women's sexual freedom to limit myself."

Pretending we're having sex because it's our right to do so is another lie women tell themselves to continue abandoning themselves for "love."

When you're done answering these questions, be sure to share them with your Mental Health Village.

You can ask your Higher Power to make you aware of when you're justifying self-destructive behavior.

Dating Rule #5: Wait to have sex. Be your own chaperone!

This is the follow-up to Dating Rule #4. Get your sex organs to simmer down before selecting a mate.

How long is long enough?

I think if I could've waited 10 to 15 dates sans sex, I never would've been drawn into my toxic relationships.

By the fifth or sixth date my guys were already unreliable and inconsistent, but since we'd already connected sexually, I was hooked.

I understand that it's easy to say, 'Wait to have Sex," but that it's actually quite difficult to pull off.

We live in a sexually free society with few boundaries, so when we date and know we want to do things differently than before …

We Have to Make a Conscious Not-So-Fast Sex Game Plan!

Some people quit their habits easily. They can go cold turkey when it comes to sex and love addiction.

But for we mere mortals, telling ourselves we *can't* eat the cake makes us rush out and eat three helpings. So, we've got to get to the bottom of *why* we can't make a decision about sex and stick with it.

There are many different paths.

Task D: **Answer these extra questions from SLAA that my client Callie answered prior to dating again after her divorce.**

Callie has kindly allowed me to share her answers:

1. Do you make promises to yourself or rules for yourself concerning your sexual or romantic behavior that you find you cannot follow?

"In the past I never made promises to myself about sex because I assumed I was *going* to have sex on the first date. I only go out with guys that I'm physically attracted to. In fact, I'm usually the one who initiates."

2. Have you had or *do* you have sex with someone you don't (didn't) want to have sex with?

"Yes! Before I was married a close friend asked me if I'd be willing to sleep with her friends' 18-year-old son because he was going through an awkward phase and needed a confidence boost.

"I did it, thinking I was helping someone. But afterwards I felt really mad at my friend for putting me in that position and even madder at myself for not saying no!"

3. Do you feel that your only (or major) value in a relationship is your ability to perform sexually, or provide an emotional fix?

"I worry if I'm not good in bed my guy will cheat on me. So, I try very hard to be sexually pleasing."

4. Have you ever wished you could stop or control your sexual and romantic activities for a given period of time?

"Yes. I've gone from one relationship to the next since I was fifteen. In fact, I get out of relationships usually by starting another one."

Callie is currently single. She is enjoying her time alone and the lack of drama as she works to change her dating/relationship patterns.

After you answer these questions share your findings with your Mental Health Village.

Task E: Attend at least six different SLAA meetings before you determine whether the program is or *isn't* right for you.

Task F: Take a break from the dating scene for six months!

After my final soul-incinerating relationship ended I made a vow *to me* that I wouldn't date for *six months*. I knew I had some stuff to figure out.

I *did* make five months completely man-free (progress, not perfection) and I worked my Twelve Step program like a stevedore.

If you want to break your toxic relationship cycle take yourself off the market for a while and work on your stuff. Or at the very least, have your first 10 to 15 dates in public.

That means no "dinner" at his or your place where you plan to lie on the couch "watching a movie" together.

Stay out of places where sex can happen until you get a sense of who this person is and whether you're compatible in all the most important ways.

Don't Spend the Next Five Years Finding Out That <u>Sex</u> Is the Only Thing This Bloke Has to Offer.

<u>Dating Rule #6</u>: Give the regular guy a chance.

I have a friend who doesn't date. Ever. The men out there are either too short or too round.

They're too too hairy or too hairless, too flabby or too skinny, too smart or too dumb … well, you get my point.

One day I exasperatedly asked, "So who would be good enough for you to date?"

Without missing a beat, she said, "Chris Hemsworth."

I'm going to leave you with that for just a moment. Chris. Hemsworth. Well, who the hell *wouldn't* want to date Chris Hemsworth?

Reality check, he falls for women like his wife Elsa, who is a cross between Jennifer Lawrence and *Venus on the Half Shell.*

Sometimes we *say* we want to date people like Chris Hemsworth and that no other lowly mortal man will do, because we're freaking *terrified* of Real Love and commitment.

We know that Chris Hemsworth is never going to come swashbuckling into our lives brandishing his "hammer." So, we never have to risk being vulnerable.

We can stay safely in our single codependent cocoon. And the fact is: That's perfectly fine.

Who says everybody has to have a significant other? Where is it written that this is the only way to feel fulfilled and happy? Not in this book, that's for sure.

But. If we really *do* want romantic love we've *got* to start picking men, not movie stars.

My husband wasn't as tall or macho as my former heartbreakers. He wasn't as brawny and didn't feel as entitled to female worship.

But as time goes by, I've realized that he's way out of my league in maturity, kindness, intelligence and humor.

And compared to my former beaux, he has a much, much bigger … heart.

There are myriad good men out there who can love us respectfully, consistently and with passion.

And once we're able to let that love in, they are no longer too short, too round, too hairy, too hairless, too flabby, too skinny.

They are, quite simply, ours.

Recap of Exercise Twelve: Follow This Dating Map to Invite Real Love

Task A: Go where the Real Love is. Seek out the company of the people who love and support you unconditionally.

Task B: Use the affirmations you've written in previous chapters to reprogram your Man-Picker.

Tasks C and D: Answer all the Sex & Love Addiction questions and describe how they manifest in your life.

Task E: Attend at least six SLAA meetings before you determine whether or not this program is for you.

Task F: Take a break from the dating scene for six months if you're single or don't go on dates in locations where sex can happen.

You've Done It!

You've reached the end of the exercises portion of this book! By now you have a journal full of revelations and inspiration.

Now is a good time to set your journal aside for a while. Let the things that you've learned settle, because you are probably on information overload.

But never fear. Everything that you've learned is stored in your subconscious now and is working on you *even as you sleep.*

In the meantime, incorporate as many of the lifestyle changes you've adopted into your current life.

These include having fun, developing a day-to-day relationship with a Higher Power, getting out of isolation and interacting with your Mental Health Village, reading your affirmations and encouraging yourself as you work to invite Real Love into your life.

MY LOVE STORY

My reader, Dana, left this comment on my relationship site shannoncolleary.com:

> "'Mister C.H. decided to move out of our house in the winter of 1997. On May 27th, 2001 I married Michael and we've never looked back.'
>
> "I wanna read the stuff between these two dates!?!? How did it all come together? I wanna hear the love story!!!!!"

So, this chapter is for Dana, and for anyone else who might be struggling to connect with a Higher Power of their own understanding in the hopes of finding Real Love.

I met Michael when I was in the thick of my relationship with Mister C.H.

I'd enrolled in a creative writing course at UCLA in the hopes of finding a distraction from my Asshat and Michael was my instructor.

Until I met Michael I never thought I was bad at picking men, just unlucky.

I surmised that there was no way to know whether a man was good or toxic until it was too late and I was already sucked in.

But I knew immediately, the way you know you've got the right pair of jeans in the dressing room, that Michael was a good man.

First, because while shooting his network television pilot in New Orleans he flew back every Wednesday on his own dime to teach. He did this, he said, because he'd "made a commitment" to his class.

Say what? Men can be that conscientious??

And second, he was immune to my flirting. One night Michael arrived late to class, a little flushed and panting.

"Just back from a rendezvous with a former student?" I queried impertinently.

"More like a rendezvous with a flu germ. You better keep your distance," he replied, deftly putting me back in my place as his pupil.

One night after class Michael asked all his students who needed a ride to their cars. (We all parked off-campus a half-mile down Sunset Boulevard to save ourselves from the exorbitant UCLA parking fees.)

That night I was the only one who needed a ride.

"Isn't there anybody else?" Michael asked in a high-pitched voice. "Anybody, anybody, anybody else??"

There was nobody else.

I detected a thin sheen of perspiration on Michael's upper lip as we embarked on the journey to the garage and his vehicle wherein we would soon be alone.

"So … I think your work is progressing," he intoned professorially. "But it's important you write scenes, write dialogue, let us see the characters outside your protagonist's head. She's interesting, but a little narcissistic …"

He was yammering. I yammered back.

"I could change her, I could make her a social worker instead of an actress. Or a missionary ... a social worker who goes on a mission?"

Were we both actually nervous?

Michael stepped up to his SUV and held open the passenger door for me. That morning I'd held the car door open for Mister C.H.

Then Michael did something that startled me. He reached across me to fasten my seatbelt.

"Sometimes it sticks," he explained.

"Thanks," I said, quick tears thickening my throat. For the first time in the longest time I felt safe.

As I stood on the curb by my car after Michael dropped me off and watched his taillights disappear, my hand lingering in its farewell salute, I had the odd sensation of being untethered from a lifeline.

One year later my family gathered at UCLA to watch a scene performed from a script I'd written.

Only five MFA screenwriting students were being given this honor and I was one of them. It was a big deal.

Even though I hadn't seen him in months, Michael agreed to introduce me before the audience of 350 Hollywood insiders.

This, despite the fact a huge action film he'd written was opening the following day.

Meanwhile, Mister C.H. balked at attending.

I had to deploy my most convincing tactics to get him there. (Except for putting a severed horse's head at the base of his bed like Don Corleone would've done.)

I introduced him to Michael on arrival. "You must be really proud of Shannon," Michael said.

"Yeah, I guess," Mister C.H. shrugged. "I hope she sells this screenplay so she can send me on a surf trip to the Canary Islands."

At the time I didn't think that was selfish.

When Michael took the podium, he pulled a wadded piece of paper from his shirt pocket.

"Today I feel like a proud father introducing his talented daughter to the writing community," he said (although he's only five years my senior FYI).

Then he spoke about my writing the way I'd always wished a man would speak about me as a woman, with love, respect and admiration.

I looked at Mister C.H. sitting next to me — his large, infuriating, handsome face — and thought, "Why am I with this person?"

Then I gazed up at Michael, with his boyish face and rumpled jacket. I suddenly heard a "voice" say, "*That* man is your husband."

I'd been working Steps Two and Three in recovery at the time. I felt certain – and am still slightly sheepish to say – that it was my Higher Power's voice.

For the next year, while trying to get Mister C.H. to propose, I often wrote in my journal, in the tone of someone confusedly scratching her own head, "I think Michael Colleary is meant to be my husband."

When Mister C.H. moved out and I finally quit him for good, I let our dogs (aka our "practice children") sleep beside me in bed, even though they shed copiously.

In their sleep, they chased rabbits while I chased my demons, the three of us twitching and snarling.

I threw away everything Mister C.H. had ever given me then casually (aka frantically) did a little recon on Michael.

It turned out he was dating an actress Who-Shall-Not-Be-Named.

She worked on television, not as a waitress at *Salt of the Sea Seafood* restaurant, like me.

One night, after work and still wearing my crab-splattered apron, I settled in with a pint of Haagen Daz Dolce de Leche, inadvertently flipping to the girlfriend's television show.

In her role as a respected neurosurgeon, she wore a skin tight, blood-besmirched sweater encasing what could only be enhanced breasts.

I hadn't thought Michael was the kind of man attracted to such extravagant breasts.

I'd thought he was too serious, and determined that perhaps I'd been mistaken and that he was most likely *not* right for me, a woman of much smaller, more tasteful breasts.

So, it was odd I dreamt that night that Michael was marrying the buxom thespian and I showed up at his wedding in San Francisco, inexplicably, wandering down the aisle wearing white, muttering "It's me, it's me, *Mother-of-God it's me!*"

The next morning, I called Michael and had a half-hour conversation about the movie business in order to ask in a croak:

"So, uh, are you … going to marry your girlfriend?"

A cryptic laugh. "That'll never happen. We broke up two weeks ago."

The Hallelujah Chorus resounded in my brain.

Next I informed every person from our former writing class that I wanted to date Michael in the hopes someone would rat me out.

No one did. It was the one time I wished people would be more indiscreet.

Five months later, a still-single me had an interview for a screen-writing job with a development executive who knew Michael.

"He's *such* husband material," she confided.

"I know," I shrieked, "I've had a kind of school-girl crush on him for some time."

"Oh my God … I'll call him. He's *crazy* not to date you."

"No, no, don't call him," I cried, twisting the top of her Evian bottle off and on. It was like Pioneer Junior High at the lockers all over again.

"I won't say you said anything, I'll just *suggest* he date you. Like *I* thought of it."

Michael phoned a week later. "So, I hear you met Susan Nesmith," he said.

"I guess she must have told you that I want to date you?"

A long pause.

"Uh ... no. Just that she *met* you."

I tried to think of some way to take it back, but nothing came to me. Nothing ever comes to me until three days later at 2 a.m.

"I always thought we should date," I finally said.

There was an exponentially longer pause wherein I heard him formulating some kind of rejection. I was right.

"Shannon, I really value this friendship, I mean, it's very important to me and I don't want to ruin it," he said.

"Oh, right, well okay."

"I mean, right now you have me up on this pedestal, I'm this revered mentor and if we date, then, you know, you'll see ... well, things will change ..."

He's afraid, I thought, *just like me.*

"I don't want to ruin our friendship either, but Michael, there might be something more special here that we're passing up. I'm willing to risk our friendship, but if you're not, I understand."

I'd never been so rational, like an accountant. Or a dental hygienist.

"But didn't you recently get out of a long-term relationship? I mean don't you need time to recover?"

"I'm already dating," I lied.

"You *are? Who?*"

"It's not important, it's just ... I'm not the kind of girl who stays on the market long."

This sounded confident. It wasn't. I was the "kind of girl" who followed her sex organs into Asshat-halla.

There was an awful silence. I never did get the screenwriting job, but Michael picked me up for our first date the following Saturday.

In deference to my in-laws I won't say the exact date we became lovers, but I will tell you that I grew to like, then care for and then love my husband over the course of two years and seven months and knew, without a doubt, that he was my perfect mate the day we wed.

GRATITUDE FOR MY ASSHATS

When we're in a toxic relationship, gratitude is a powerful tool for hope, reminding us of the many blessings we *still* have.

So, it can seem odd to express gratitude for the toxic relationship itself.

But I suggest you try just that — AFTER you've put a big, healthy distance between yourself and the Heartbreaker.

Gratitude is empowering. It helps us detach with love. It also helps us forgive others *and* ourselves.

Gratitude relieves us of the toxic resentments we've been polishing like fine gems that are *actually* bison dung and keep us miserable.

In that spirit, I'd like to express the gratitude I *now* have for both The Greek God and Mister Cruelly Handsome, because both of those relationships had positive moments of love, understanding and connection.

To My College Sweetheart

I am so grateful:

* You were my first love.
* That you pretended to give me a cigarette lighter (even though I didn't smoke) on the first birthday we spent together, then surprised me with a beautiful gold chain.
* That our love song was Chicago's, *"You're My Inspiration."*
* That you wrote, "I Love You" in a carrot with your fingernail and covertly showed it to me during a tense family gathering.
* That you taught me to water-ski and gave me so many lazy, sunny days on the stunning Colorado River.
* That you didn't drink or do drugs and made it easy for me to avoid them throughout my college years.
* That you wrote me such beautiful, heartsick letters when I was on my semester abroad.
* That your wonderful family made me feel like I was one of their own.
* That in the end you were faithful and trustworthy while I drifted away.

Thank you for being my first love. And although our relationship was painful for me at times, I feel certain you've gone on to become a dedicated husband and father.

To My Last Long-Term Beau

* Thank you for encouraging me to go back to school to change my career.
* Thank you for always telling me I was beautiful.
* Thank you for introducing me to the melodic stylings of Sade.

* Thank you for paying more than your share when we lived together those last two years.
* Thank you for that one glorious night of dancing where we both let our guard down and laughed together like friends.
* Thank you for showing me what it means to be a loving uncle by caring for your young nieces and nephew when I had no interest in helping take care of my nieces and nephews at all.
* Thank you for always believing in me as a creative person and an artist.

Although our relationship was often painful for me, it's my hope you've found love and happiness.

A FAREWELL TO ARMS

I t appears we've come to the end of this book.

My hope is that it's the beginning of a new life for you, one with greater depth, self-honesty, intimacy and connection.

Beginning recovery can be frightening. When we look behind us everything we once knew might be turned to smoldering ash.

When we turn to look ahead of us we may not see a clear path to a happier future. It's as if one of those scary Stephen King mists full of bogeymen has fallen before us.

In the course of one year I gave up acting and Asshats.

I had no idea what might move in to fill the void, but I knew I could *not* go back to life as it once was, even if I wanted to.

So I "acted as if" I had faith in my Higher Power and stood very still, awaiting directions.

The mist didn't suddenly clear and reveal a path to the horizon. Instead, just an inch of road appeared. And I stepped forward.

And that's pretty much the way my recovery has been ever since. One inch at a time, one step at a time, one day at a time.

Thanks for coming on this journey with me and now I leave you to the grace and beauty of your own recovery.

In the words of a truly wise shaman:

"May *The Force* Be with You" -- Jedi Master Obi-Wan Kenobi

LITERARY RESOURCES

You need this stuff!

I suggest you add the following books to your night table stack. In no particular order they are:

* *Codependent No More: How to Stop Controlling Others and Start Caring for Yourself* by Melody Beattie
* *The Language of Letting Go: Daily Meditations for Codependents* by Melody Beattie.
* *Codependent's Guide to the Twelve Steps* by Melody Beattie
* *Co-Dependents Anonymous* by Coda
* *Drop The Rock* by Bill P. Todd W. and Sarah S.
* *The Magic* by Rhonda Byrne
* *Men Who Can't Love* by Steven Carter & Julia Sokol
* *Homecoming: Reclaiming and Healing Your Inner Child* by John Bradshaw
* *You Are a Badass: How to Stop Doubting Your Greatness and Start Living an Awesome Life* by Jen Sincero
* *The Twelve Steps and Twelve Traditions* by Alcoholics Anonymous

* *Courage to Change: One Day at a Time in Al-Anon II*
* *You Can Heal Your Life* by Louise L Hay
* *The War of Art* by Stephen Pressfield (for those of us in an abusive relationship with our creativity).

If you'd like to stay informed of my programs, webinars, seminars and conferences be sure to opt-in to my biweekly relationship newsletter at http://eepurl.com/bnjmyT

You can also follow me on Twitter @ShannonColleary or on Facebook at http://www.facebook.com/s.colleary.

If you found this book helpful I'd be ever so grateful if you would leave a review on the platform you purchased it.

I look forward to catalyzing and helping as many women as I can to skip the heartbreakers and invite Real Love.

xo S

Made in the USA
Charleston, SC
28 January 2017